Fashion

Color, Line, and Design
Third Edition

Fashion

Color, Line, and Design
Third Edition

Susan Geringer

GLENCOE PUBLISHING COMPANY
Mission Hills, California

For my husband, Steve

Acquisition and Development Editor:	Patricia K. Parrott
Associate Editor:	Mary Powers
Editorial and Production Management:	Visual Education Corporation
Project Manager:	Maureen Ryan
Cover and Text Designer:	Arthur Ritter
Editors:	Rita Bernhardt, Stephanie Levy, Alice Calaprice, Karen Sardinas-Wyssling
Production Coordinator:	Paula Harris
Artists:	Max Crandall, Jim Edwards
Cover Photographer:	Tom Dunham

ABOUT THE AUTHOR: Susan Geringer (M.A. Education) is a lecturer in Textiles, Clothing, and Fashion Merchandising at California State University, Sacramento, and at American River College. She has retail buying and management experience with large and small retailers, including Macy's of California.

Send all inquiries to:
Glencoe Publishing Company
15319 Chatsworth Street
Mission Hills, California 91345

Library of Congress Cataloging in Publications Data

Geringer, Susan.
  Fashion color, line, and design.
  Includes index.
  1. Fashion. 2. Clothing trade. I. Title.
TT518.G47 1985   746.9'2   85-22009

Fashion: Color, Line, and Design, 2nd Edition by Leslie Peltz

Printed in the United States of America

ISBN 0-02-682880-4 (Student Text)
ISBN 0-02-682890-1 (Instructor's Guide)

3   4   5   6   7   8   9   91   90   89   88

Glencoe Publishing Company
Fashion Merchandising Series

Fashion Accessories, 3rd Edition, by Leslie Peltz

Fashion Color, Line, and Design, 3rd Edition, by Susan Geringer

Fashion Direction and Coordination, 2nd Edition, by Susan Goschie

Fashion Textiles and Laboratory Workbook, 3rd Edition, by Robert J. Beaulieu

Fashion Writing, 2nd Edition, by Mimi Drennan

(An Instructor's Guide accompanies each text.)

Fashion Board of Consultants

Jacqueline Cole
City Technical Institute

Lenore Eisenstein
Los Angeles Trade-Technical College

Jacqueline Geiss
American Business and Fashion Institute

Eve Pollack
Fashion Institute of Technology

Jack J. Rose
Fashion Institute of Fort Lauderdale

Sylvia Sheppard
The Fashion Institute of Design and Merchandising

Contents

3
Design Lines and Principles

4
Fashion Drawing

5
History of Costume

Introduction

The world of fashion is an exciting world of change. In your fashion career, you'll need to recognize and predict trends, and this text will help you do so. It will introduce you to the basics of color, silhouette, design, fashion drawing, historical costumes, and fashion designers. It isn't intended as a "how-to" manual on designing clothing, but rather as a source book providing a basic understanding of the fashion industry.

Knowledge of color theory is important in the study of fashion. In clothing and accessories, color may be more influential than styling details when it comes to making a sale. It takes practice to develop the eye for color that's needed by a buyer, coordinator, designer, fashion writer, or sales consultant. Knowing how to mix colors will help you recognize the casts of a color. Green, for example, can have a bluish cast. Knowing how to mix colors will also help you describe colors clearly when writing reports and articles. This text will also teach you the basics of color theory.

To describe fashions clearly and accurately, you must be familiar with styling terms and you must be able to recognize details of garments and accessories. This text will give you the terminology of styling details, silhouette, color, and fabric so you can write fashion reports for stores, buying offices, magazines, newspapers, and manufacturers.

Two chapters deal with design. Design lines and principles are shown in relation to fashion design. An understanding of the principles of design will help you recognize well-designed, marketable fashion garments.

The ability to draw a well-proportioned fashion figure is an important asset. The illustration need not be perfect, just well-proportioned. Traditionally, designs for each season emphasize a particular area of the female figure—for example, the legs or the waistline. Designs for men also emphasize a particular area of the body. Wherever the emphasis is placed, the proportion of the body stays fairly constant. This text will teach you how to draw basic fashion figures.

The design of garments or accessories involves the combination of proportion, color, texture, and silhouette. Most of the silhouettes have a historical basis. Over the centuries, styles have been adapted and readapted to reflect the attitudes and events of the times. This text will explore the evolution of costume from 4500 B.C. to the present.

Fashion designers throughout the years have reflected the times through their creations. Many designers achieve success because of their ability to interpret current events and the desires of consumers. This text will feature some of the world's most prominent and influential designers and their contributions to the fashion industry.

In summary, after studying this text, you will have a knowledge of color theory, familiarity with styling terminology, a technique for drawing a well-proportioned fashion figure, an awareness of historical fashion, and a recognition of fashion designers. Each of these will contribute to your knowledge and enjoyment of the fashion industry.

Fashion

Color, Line, and
Design
Third Edition

1
Color

A store advertises a red sweater. Do you think of tomatoes, strawberries, blood, a fire engine? Do certain colors make you happy and others make you sad? Do you have a favorite color? Why is it your favorite? The eye beholds color, and the mind interprets the sensations received. Everyone, therefore, perceives colors differently.

COLOR PSYCHOLOGY AND SYMBOLISM

Everyone responds to color and has definite preferences. Many studies of people and their responses to color have been done, giving rise to certain generalities. The most-liked color is blue, followed by red, then by green, violet, orange, and yellow. Light colors are usually preferred over dark ones, as are primaries over intermediates, and pure hues over grayed ones. Introverts generally prefer neutral colors (beige, brown, tan, gray, black, and white), while extroverts generally prefer bright ones. Neutral colors are considered to be more sophisticated. People who live in hot climates generally prefer cool colors (blue, green, and purple) because they reflect light and heat. In cold climates, people choose warm colors (red, yellow, and orange) because they attract light and heat.

Numerous researchers have studied the psychological effects of colors. One study shows that babies react to bold, bright colors and show a preference for red.[1] Certain colors have been associated with specific forms of mental illnesses, particularly red with manic tendencies, green with psychosis, and blue with schizophrenia.[2] Blood pressure and respiratory rate can be increased under red light and decreased under blue light.[3]

People have become increasingly conscious of color, partly because of the large number of color analysts who are employed today. These analysts have brought color to the consumer's attention.

Colors have symbolic meanings and evoke definite individual reactions. Because of the significance of first impressions, it is important for you to understand that the color of your clothing sends out definite nonverbal messages about yourself.

Favorite colors tend to reflect the personality. Red is positive, energetic, impulsive, and fits an outgoing person. Orange is exciting and glowing. Yellow, the most luminous color, is cheerful, creative, and intellectual, but is also least liked, sometimes being associated with sickness and cowardice. Blue, the most popular color, is calming, peaceful, and conservative. Green is fresh and restful; it is the color of grass and plants, but it is also associated with jealousy. Violet is cooling, but tends to be gloomy; it has been associated with older women. Purple is also soothing, though richer than violet; it is often associated with royalty. White is airy, and sometimes cold; it implies innocence and is the traditional bridal color in the United States (Figure

Figure 1–1
White, the traditional bridal color, continues to be popular for wedding gowns.   Reprinted from Bride's Copyright
© 1985 by The Condé Nast Publications, Inc.

Figure 1–2
This evening gown, designed by Mr. Blackwell,
epitomizes the sophistication associated with black.
Original sketch courtesy of Mr. Blackwell.

COLOR AND FASHION

Color is an important part of fashion apparel. The colors in an apparel line can be as significant as the silhouettes. Designers carefully choose their fabric colorations to make definite statements, sometimes using one color throughout a line and other times using a coloration for groups in a line. Colors combined for use in prints must harmonize either in a classical or in an unorthodox way. Sometimes a particular designer's unusual combination becomes a standard that other designers adopt.

Traditionally, color has had seasonal associations. Dark and rich colors were designated for fall and winter, while pale and pastel colors were designated for spring and summer. Now wardrobes have become less seasonal, and the use of color is less restricted. White, beigy neutrals, and misty pastels appear in winter apparel collections. Bright, bold, hot colors are seen throughout the year. Navy, black, and brown are seen in both summer-weight fabrics and in winter wools.

The photos on pages 5 and 6 display some of the color choices available in today's apparel collections.

Contemporary menswear has generally been less changeable than women's wear. Black, navy, gray, brown, and camel at one time were practically the only colors available to men. Recently, though, more colors have been appearing in menswear collections. Contemporary designers recognized the void in colors available to men. They now make shirts, ties, sweaters, socks, and shoes in colors to coordinate with a suit or slacks, and sportjacket. Colors normally dominate men's sportswear, and many men have shirts ranging from classic white to bold, multicolored prints. Today's fashion-conscious man also has a choice of colors for his underwear.

Another apparel area that has blossomed in color is active sportswear for both men and women. Both participants and spectators now wear an array of bright colors. Color in the tiniest bikini or in a slick tank suit livens up pools and beaches all over the world. Tennis club members may still prefer traditional white on the courts, but they choose colors for trims,

1–1). Black can be fearful or formal; it can mean terror or evil and, in the United States, is often associated with mourning. In the twentieth century, black has come to be associated with sophistication, as in the black velvet evening gown designed by Mr. Blackwell (Figure 1–2). Gray is sedate, cold, and quiet. Brown is considered earthy, but is liked by people with a sophisticated eye.

Colors have varying connotations. A blue, green, or pale violet room is restful. A red room is stimulating. Pale blue is associated with baby boys and pale pink with baby girls. A red light means stop, and a green one, go. Yellow-orange means caution.

Colors are also used to reflect mood. People tend to wear bright colors to call attention to themselves when they are in a pleasant mood. They wear dark, somber colors when they are in a bad mood and wish to be left alone.

Figure 1–4
Color has traditionally had seasonal associations. This Ter Bantine design uses autumn gold in a design for that season.

Figure 1–3
Perry Ellis has carefully chosen fabric and color in this fashion. Rich, dark colors have been used in harmony.
Courtesy of Perry Ellis Sportswear.

Figure 1–5
Today designers combine colors and prints in unusual ways. While the colors in this design suggest winter, Yves Saint Laurent uses a plaid skirt with a print blouse to create a new impact.

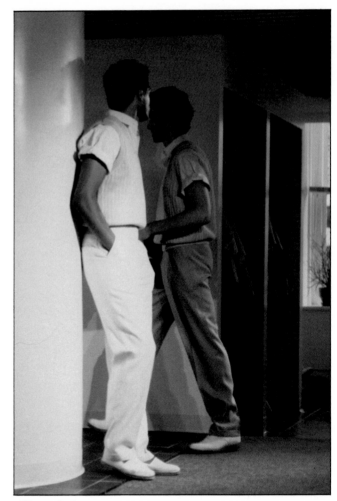

Figure 1–6
Contemporary designers include more color in menswear collections. Liz Claiborne coordinates pastels in these designs.
Courtesy of Liz Claiborne, Inc.

Color Wheel

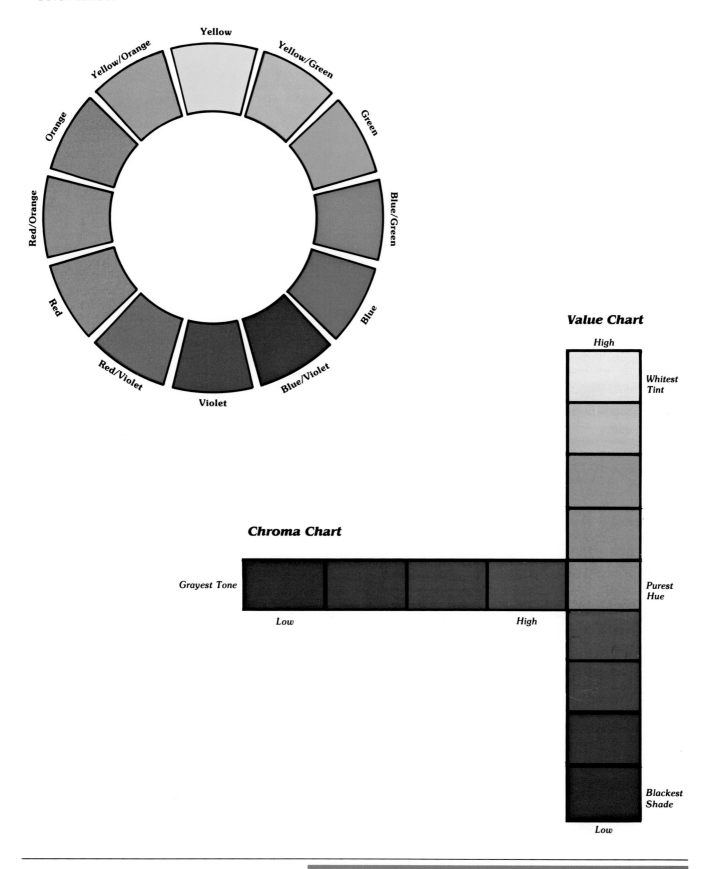

Yellow

Yellow/Orange

Yellow/Green

Orange

Green

Red/Orange

Blue/Green

Red

Blue

Red/Violet

Blue/Violet

Violet

Value Chart

High

Whitest Tint

Purest Hue

Blackest Shade

Low

Chroma Chart

Grayest Tone

Low

High

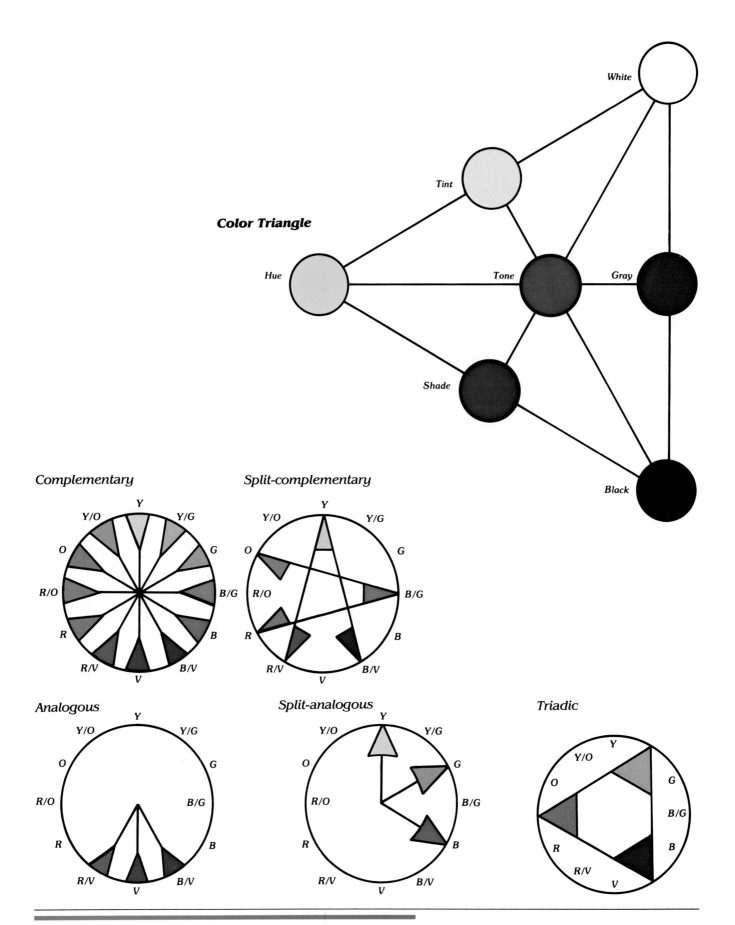

Color Triangle

Complementary

Split-complementary

Analogous

Split-analogous

Triadic

jackets, and accessories. Physical fitness used to bring to mind the image of runners wearing drab sweat suits. Now the image is of hills, trails, streets, and tracks inundated with clear, bright colors on the move. Ski slopes are vibrant with color, from brightly colored ski suits to caps, goggles, and boots.

Coordinating the colors of accessories to clothing is another important aspect of fashion. Cosmetic companies regularly introduce new colors to their product lines to go with the colors shown in that season's fashions. Eyeglass manufacturers have also taken color seriously, since many people have a selection of frames to coordinate with their wardrobe. Today, people can even change their eye color by using tinted contact lenses. Color doesn't stop at cosmetics and eyewear, of course. It's used in such accessories as hosiery, belts, handbags, jewelry, scarves, and shoes.

Many people deal with color in their professions. Fashion designers choose color schemes for their lines, then work with textile houses to obtain the required colors and fabrics. Mass-market apparel manufacturers often employ stylists who choose the fabrics and color schemes. Textile manufacturers, fiber producers, yarn producers, and leather companies all employ colorists who foresee trends and choose the colors that will go into the company's products. Those who work in textiles, fibers, and yarns generally work two years in advance of the season. They make color swatch cards twice a year, in the fall/winter and spring/summer seasons, in the colors that they consider important for the future season. The colors of these swatch cards are well researched and carefully developed. The colorist or stylist usually chooses a theme, and the colors are then named to fit that theme. For example, a "spice" theme may be used with colors such as nutmeg, cinnamon, paprika, or ginger.

Information about color can be obtained from color prediction associations, such as Inter-Color. It is made up of colorists throughout the world, who meet in Paris twice a year to predict the color story approximately two years in advance. The participating colorists then return to their countries and interpret their color findings to suit the tastes of their country's fashion consumers.

It is costly and impractical for a producer to change all colors each season. Some colors, such as white, black, navy, and beige, are basic and are repeated successfully over many seasons. Other colors, such as cranberry, have a life of only a few seasons. A successful dark color in winter can be a successful accent color in spring and summer. Each season builds on the season before it.

Color is not simple. It is all around us in many forms. It permeates every part of life. Many people even dream in color. Experiment with mixing pigments and coordinating the colors in your wardrobe. It is essential for retail display artists to have a complete understanding of color usage so they can better merchandise their company's products.

COLOR TERMS

A knowledge of basic color language will help you discuss and understand color. A few basic terms will be defined before theories of color are discussed.

Pigment   Dry coloring matter to be mixed with water, oil, or another base to produce paint, dye, or ink.

Primaries   The three basic colors—red, blue, and yellow—that are equidistant from each other on the color wheel (see page 7). All other colors are derived from the primaries.

Secondaries   Colors that are equal combinations of the primaries. In pigments, yellow and red equals orange, red and blue equals violet, and blue and yellow equals green. Orange, violet, and green are secondaries (see the color wheel).

Intermediates   Colors that are combinations of a primary and a secondary. In pigments, yellow and orange equals yellow-orange, red and orange equals red-orange, red and violet equals red-violet, blue and violet equals blue-violet, blue and green equals blue-green, and yellow and green equals yellow-green. Yellow-orange, red-orange, red-violet, blue-violet, blue-green, and yellow-green are intermediates (see color wheel).

Hue A pure color, including the primaries, secondaries, and intermediates. Any color that doesn't have white, black, or gray added to it. Hue is also the name of the color as it appears on the color wheel. This name may not always correspond with the fashion color name.

Tint The color achieved by adding white to a hue.

Shade The color achieved by adding black to a hue.

Tone The color achieved by adding gray to a hue.

Value The lightness or darkness of a color as determined by the amount of black or white added to it. A high value color has a great deal of white in it; a low value color has a great deal of black. Value is measured on a vertical chart beginning with the blackest shade on bottom, the purest hue generally in the middle, and the whitest tint on the top (see value chart on page 7).

Chroma The intensity of a color as determined by the amount of gray in it. A color of high chroma is almost pure; a color of low chroma has a great deal of gray in it. Chroma is measured on a horizontal scale, right to left, beginning with the purest hue and ending with its grayest tone. Chroma is also called saturation (see chroma chart on page 7).

Chromatic colors Colors with a hue in them. They can be altered by adding other hues, black, white, or gray.

Achromatic colors The colors black, white, and gray. They can be made darker or lighter by adding black, white, or gray.

COLOR THEORY

In 1666 Sir Isaac Newton identified color in light. He used a glass prism to **refract** (break) a ray of light into violet, blue, green, yellow, orange, and red. The band of color formed in this way is called the **spectrum.** The colors of the spectrum have different **wavelengths.** To get a picture of "wavelength," imagine a rolling wave. The distance between the crests of two waves next to each other is the wavelength. Red has the longest wavelength, violet has the shortest, and the wavelengths of the other colors are in between. You can see the spectrum when the sun's rays are refracted by raindrops, and a rainbow is formed.

Newton recognized a relationship between spectrum red and spectrum violet. He formed the first color circle based on the red and violet relationship. The colors extending from red toward violet on his circle are orange, yellow, green, blue, and indigo.

Much study and theorizing have been done since Newton devised his circle of color, or color wheel. Theories about primary colors generally fall into three categories: 1) color in light, 2) color in vision, and 3) color in pigment.

The first theory, devised in 1790, falls into the category of color in light. The primaries are red, green, and blue-violet. In light, red and green equals yellow; green and blue-violet equals turquoise; red and blue-violet equals magenta. Light mixture is **additive,** meaning when the three primaries are mixed, they produce white light. Albert H. Munsell, American colorist famous at the beginning of the twentieth century, based his color wheel on this theory, although his principle hues were red, yellow, green, blue, and purple.

The second theory belongs in the category of color in vision and was established by a German physiologist, Ewald Hering, in 1874. In vision there are four primary hues—red, yellow, green, and blue. Vision mixture is **medial,** meaning when these primaries are mixed, they produce gray. Hering's theory was the basis for Wilhelm Ostwald's color wheel, established in the early twentieth century. Ostwald's primaries were red, yellow, sea green, and blue. Ostwald also set up a color triangle (see page 8). Using this triangle, you can see the changes that a hue goes through with the addition of black, white, and gray. A hue such as yellow, preferably a primary or secondary, is at one corner. Black and white each form a corner. Lines connect the three colors. Gray rests on the line halfway between black and white. A shade (of yellow) rests on the line halfway between yellow and black. A tint (of yellow) rests on the line halfway between yellow and white. A tone (of yellow) is in the center of the triangle, and three lines run through it, one between yellow and gray, one between the tint and black, and one between the shade and white.

The third theory of primary colors is based on the combination of pigments (paints, dyes, or inks) and was devised by J. C. LeBlon in 1730. Red, yellow, and blue are the primaries. Pigment mixture is **subtractive,** meaning when the primaries are mixed, they produce black or dark brown.

Primary red, blue, and yellow have many variations, and thus color circles (also color triangles, stars, and solids), though based on the primaries red, blue, and yellow, have differed through the years. The traditional color circle has a clear yellow, a crimson red, and a cobalt blue. The circle devised by Herbert E. Ives, which is commonly used for printing, has a clear yellow, a magenta red, and a turquoise blue.

COLOR SCHEMES

It is possible to make many colors by mixing the three primaries, but better variation and wider range of intensity are achieved when more colors are used. To mix a fairly complete palette, the following pigments are suggested: cadmium or spectrum yellow, vermilion or spectrum red, turquoise blue, ultra-marine blue, purple, black, and white.

In developing color schemes it is important to realize that color can produce varying effects. The goal is usually to have a harmonious combination of colors that is pleasing to the eye. The following are some general principles regarding combination of colors. All pure hues generally look good with the addition of white or black. A hue with its tints and white produces a soft effect, one which was often used by the Impressionists.[4] A hue with its shades and blacks produces a rich effect, used by the Old Masters.[5] Tint, tone, and shade harmonies result in a shadowy effect. Gray works well with such harmonies. Tints look good with white, shades with black, and

tones with gray. Tints of light intensity hues (yellow, orange) look best, and shades of dark intensity hues (blue, violet) look best. Tints, tones, and black, or shades, tones, and white make other interesting combinations. Harmonious effects can also be produced by using a hue with one of its tints, shades, and tones, and white, black, and gray.

Texture can change the intensity of a color. Red satin will seem more intense than flannel in the same red. Effects of transparency, luster, luminosity, and iridescence can be produced, depending on how the color is used. An overlay of pigment can make something appear transparent. An area of color can appear lustrous if it is small and if the hue is pure and stands out in contrast to black. An area that is to appear luminous must also be small, be of strong chroma, and have overall light. Gray contrasts can create an impression of iridescence.

MORE COLOR TERMS

The following are more terms basic to the study of color.

Tertiaries Colors that are combinations of secondaries that form softened versions of primaries. In pigments, orange and violet equals a low tone of red, violet and green equals a low tone of blue, green and orange equals a low tone of yellow. These low intensity colors are tertiaries.

Warm hues Hues on the color wheel that give a feeling of warmth such as yellow, yellow-orange, orange, red-orange, and red. Red-violet and yellow-green overlap on the cool side. Warm hues are good highlighters because they tend to stand out when used in combination with other hues.

Cool hues Hues on the color wheel that give a feeling of coolness, such as violet, blue-violet, blue, blue-green, and green. Cool hues make good background colors, because they tend to recede when used in combination with other hues.

Monochromatic A color scheme based on one hue, or on combinations of the hue with its tints, tones, and shades. An example would be wearing a medium-brown jacket, chocolate brown shirt, and beige blouse at the same time.

Complementary   A color scheme made up of two hues that are opposite each other on the color wheel, such as red and green (see page 8). Complementary color schemes using primaries and secondaries are bolder than those using intermediates. A complementary color scheme sometimes includes the tints, shades, and tones of the two complements. Because of the bold nature of complementary colors, they are most commonly used in sportswear.

Split-complementary   A color scheme made up of a hue and the two hues adjacent to its complement (see page 8).

Analogous   A color scheme made up of hues that are next to each other on the color wheel. In an analogous color scheme, the best effects are produced when the middle hue is a primary or secondary and the adjacent hues are intermediates, such as yellow-orange, orange, or red-orange. By varying the tints, shades, and tones of the hue, interesting color schemes can be made (see page 8).

Split-analogous   A color scheme made up of hues that are adjacent to each other on the color wheel but that are one hue apart, such as red, violet, and blue or yellow-green, blue-green, and blue-violet (see page 8).

Triadic   A color scheme made up of three hues that are equally distant from each other on the color wheel, such as yellow, red, and blue or red-orange, blue-violet, and yellow-green. This scheme can be varied by using shades, tones, and tints of the three colors (see page 8).

Projects

1. Color Triangle
    Choose a hue from the color wheel, preferably a primary or secondary. Paint a matching swatch, then make your own color triangle.

2. Value Chart
    Choose a hue and paint a 2 × 1 inch swatch which will be placed at No. 5 position as you count vertically from the bottom of a chroma/value chart (see page 7). Add black to the hue to create shades (swatches No. 4 to No. 1); add white to the hue to create tints (swatches No. 6 to No. 9).

3. Chroma Chart
    Choose a hue and paint four different tones of the hue. A tone is a hue that is grayed by adding gray pigment, black and white, or the complement of the hue on the color wheel. Present the chart horizontally, with the pure hue on the right-hand side (see chroma/value chart on page 7).

4. Color Schemes
    On tracing paper draw an abstract design 6×6 inches. Trace the design onto white paper six times. Choose six hues and their tints, shades, and tones. Color one 6×6 inch design in each of the following color schemes: monochromatic, complementary, split-complementary, analogous, split-analogous, and triadic (see page 8).

5. Tertiaries
    Paint a color swatch for each of the tertiaries.

6. Brown Chart
    Many different paint mixtures will result in brown, for example, orange and black. Paint five 2 × 2 inch swatches of brown. Label each swatch with the names of the pigments used.

7. Original Color Circle
    Paint 12 color swatches 2 × 2 inches in the primaries, secondaries, and intermediates that will go through the primary family groups (yellow/orange/red, violet/blue/green). Before you paste down the swatches to form the circle, put them into interesting shapes.

8. Swatch Card

Design and construct a swatch card for the incoming fashion season, to be used by the manufacturer, pattern company, magazine, retail buyer, or consumer. The swatch card should include:

a. an original theme
b. color samples, using fabric, yarn, or paint
c. color names
d. a written description of color and fabric trends for the season

9. Color in Fashion

Clip two examples of each of the following uses of color in a garment from current fashion magazines:

a. monochromatics
b. two or more primaries
c. two or more secondaries
d. warm hues
e. cool hues
f. complementary colors
g. analogous colors

2
Clothing Details

Although clothing styles change from season to season, the basic elements of most garments remain the same. A designer's adaptation of these basic elements is what makes the diversity of clothing styles.

The descriptions of clothing and construction details in this chapter are standard. You will not see all of these details used every season, but they recur. A style of collar, sleeve, coat, or skirt not seen one year may be the most outstanding look the following year. It is important to know these clothing details and terminology and to be able to recognize them in order to understand and interpret fashion cycles, trends, and silhouettes.

DRESSES, SKIRTS, AND SHIRTS

A-line   In a dress, the fabric skims the waistline and flares to the hem; in a skirt, the fabric skims the hips and flares to the hem. (See Figure 2–1).

Bias   A dress made from cloth cut on the bias (see "Construction Details" later in this chapter). The figure-hugging silhouette was popularized by Madeleine Vionnet (Vee oh NAY), a French designer.

Blouson   A dress or blouse silhouette with a loose top gathered into a waistline that appears dropped. The effect, even in a dress, is that of an overblouse.

Camisole   Woman's lightweight garment worn as both a blouse and as an undergarment. It may feature thin shoulder straps or be strapless (Figure 2–2).

Chemise (shuh MEEZ)   A straight dress silhouette lacking a waistline. It was introduced in 1957 by Spanish designer Balenciaga, and is also known as a sack or a shift. It is also a loose, short slip worn as a woman's undergarment. Chemise is the French word for shirt (Figure 2–3).

Circular   A skirt that forms a circle when laid flat. It is smooth across the hips and full below.

Corselet   A dress with a tight fitting midriff that often has lacing through eyelets.

Dirndl (DURN duhl)   A full skirt featuring a gathered waist and curved side seams that eliminate some of the fullness at the hips (Figure 2–1).

Draped   Inspired by the costumes of ancient Greece, the term refers to a dress, skirt, or blouse that has fabric falling in soft folds. The neckline of a garment may be draped, as well as the shoulder or sleeve. This look was popularized by Mme. Grès, a French designer.

Dress shirt   A short- or long-sleeve man's shirt with a collar. It is generally a solid color but may be striped, checked, or patterned. It is sold by neck and sleeve length and is available in fitted, semi-fitted, and full cuts.

A-Line skirt

Dirndl skirt

Gored skirt

Figure 2–1

Figure 2–2

Dropped-waist dress   Dress design in which the bodice meets the skirt below the wearer's natural waistline (Figure 2–3).

Empire   A dress with the waistline placed below the bust. This style is often seen in maternity-wear designs. It was popularized by Empress Josephine during the French Empire period of 1804 to 1814.

Evening shirt   A man's shirt for formal attire, having long sleeves, a wing collar, and a starched front.

Fitted shirt   A style used for both men's and women's shirts, having curved seams that make the shirt hug the body. In menswear, it is also known as a European cut.

Godet (goh DAY)   A skirt with triangular inserts near the hem to add flare.

Gored   A skirt or dress with shaped panels that add fullness to the garment (Figure 2–1).

Hawaiian shirt   Tropical print lightweight shirt worn by men and women. It features a notched collar, button-front closure, and short sleeves (Figure 2–2).

Jumper A sleeveless dress without a collar that is meant to be worn over a blouse or sweater.

Kilt A short, pleated skirt adapted from the costume of the Scottish Highlanders. It is most often plaid.

Kimono (Kuh MOH nuh) The native dress of Japan, worn by both men and women. It has wide, short sleeves that are cut with the back and front of the kimono from one piece of cloth. An obi (OH bee), or wide sash, circles the waist and holds the garment together. This style is often seen in loungewear.

Man-tailored A woman's shirt styled after a man's, usually having a short-pointed collar, a button-front closing, and long sleeves with a French or button cuff.

Middy A blouse adapted from the sailor's costume, having a low waist and long sleeves with a tight cuff. It has a sailor collar, often in a contrasting color.

Mini A very short skirt or dress, with a hem at least 4 inches above the knee. It was introduced by English designer Mary Quant in 1967 and popularized again in the early 1980s.

Peplum A flared, hip-length tier attached at the waistline of a dress, coat, jacket, or blouse (Figure 2–3). It was introduced in the costumes of ancient Greek civilizations.

Petal A skirt with overlapping fabric that resembles flower petals.

Pinafore A sleeveless apron-like garment that can be worn alone or over other apparel. It often has ruffles at the shoulder. The pinafore was originally designed as a cover-up for children's clothing, but it is also used in women's apparel.

Pleated Skirts, dresses, or blouses with folds pressed or stitched in place (see "Construction Details" later in this chapter).

Polo shirt A short-sleeve knit shirt with a ribbed collar and rib trim on the sleeve (Figure 2–2). The polo shirt is worn by men, women, and children.

Princess A close-fitting dress or coat that is gored (see "Construction Details") and

has a full skirt. There is no break at the waistline. The fit of the garment is achieved by the construction lines.

Shirtdress or shirtwaist A dress adapted from a man's shirt. It has a front closing that can stop at the waist or continue to the hem, may be belted, and can be short-sleeve, long-sleeve, or sleeveless (Figure 2–3). It can also have a collar or be collarless. It is a very classic design.

Smock A loose shirt or jacket with front and back yokes, patch pockets, cuffed sleeves, and a collar. It is traditionally a peasant shirt with smocking detail (see "Construction Details") on the yoke and cuffs. It may also be used as a cover-up to protect clothing.

Sport shirt A man's short- or long-sleeve shirt worn with sporty attire. It can be brightly colored or patterned, or made in a novelty fabric. Sport shirts are sold in small, medium, large, and extra-large sizes.

Straight A slim straight-line skirt that may have a few pleats, or a slit, at the hemline for ease in moving.

Tank top An unfitted, sleeveless top with a deep U-neck.

Tiered skirt A skirt with layers of flounces.

Trapeze An exaggerated A-line style dress or coat introduced by French designer Christian Dior in 1955. Yves Saint Laurent popularized the trapeze in his 1958 collection for the House of Dior. It is often seen in maternity-wear lines.

Trumpet A skirt with pleats or godets (see "Construction Details") placed near the hem to form a flare like that of a trumpet.

T-shirt A plain, short-sleeve shirt with a crew or V-neck (see "Necklines and Collars" later in this chapter). It may be solid or multicolored and can also be worn as underwear by men and boys.

Tunic A blouse-like garment, usually with short or long sleeves. It extends to mid-thigh and may have a belt. It is often worn over a dress, a blouse and slacks, or a blouse and skirt.

Western shirt A man's or woman's tapered shirt with yoke front and back, a pointed collar, two patch pockets with flaps,

Chemise

Dropped-waist dres

Figure 2–3

Peplum

Shirt dress

and fancy snap closures on front placket, pocket, and cuffs. The yoke is often seen in a contrasting color.

Wrap-around A dress, skirt, or coat that wraps around the body. It fastens with snaps or a hidden closure rather than with buttons or a zipper, and there is usually a belt to hold it in place.

COATS, JACKETS, AND SUITS

Baseball jacket A short, snap-front jacket with knitted neck, cuffs, and bottom, and with slash pockets. Fashion baseball jackets are adapted from those worn by major league baseball teams, which were originally in two-toned fabric and embroidered with the team name and player's name.

Battle jacket A jacket adapted from those worn by men in the United States Armed Forces during World War II. It is single-breasted, banded at the waist, and has patch pockets with flaps. It is also known as an "Eisenhower jacket."

Beachcoat A man's or woman's coat or jacket, usually made of an absorbent fabric such as terry cloth, intended to be worn over bathing suits.

Blazer A jacket for men or women. It may be single- or double-breasted, solid-color or striped (Figure 2–4).

Bolero A short, above-the-waist jacket adapted from a native Spanish costume. The bolero is open in front with a curved bottom hem, with or without sleeves.

Bomber jacket A jacket adapted from those worn by the United States Navy. It is also known as a flight jacket and may be made of various fabrics, leather being very common. It features a bi-swing back, wool collar, side pockets, knit cuffs and waistband, and epaulets (Figure 2–4).

Box A straight, loose-fitting, beltless, single- or double-breasted coat for men and women.

Burnoose A loose, light-colored cloak with a hood.

Cape A sleeveless outer garment that closes at the neck and hangs over the back and shoulders. It may feature a hood and comes in various lengths and fabrics (Figure 2–5).

Cardigan A sweater, dress, jacket, or coat for men, women, or children that is collarless and buttons down the front. It can have either a round or V-neck and is usually banded around the neck and down the front.

Chanel suit A suit designed for women by French fashion designer Coco Chanel. This classic suit features a straight skirt and a short, cardigan-style jacket (Figure 2–5). The jacket is often edged with a rich braided trim known as soutache (soo TASH) trim.

Chesterfield A semifitted coat, single- or double-breasted, beltless, with flap pockets, fly front, and a contrasting velvet collar (Figure 2–5). It was originally designed for men, but is worn by women also.

Cutaway A man's formal daytime coat, cut with a curve from the front waistline to the back tails.

Directoire (dy rehk TWAHR) Coat for men and women inspired by the costumes from the French Directoire period, 1795 to 1799. It is fitted through the waist, and has a flared skirt and a high, standing collar with lapels. It is also known as a Napoleon jacket.

Duffle A boxy, knee-length sport coat of coarse, sturdy fabric, popularized in America as the loden coat. It is unlined and closes with wooden toggles and hemp loops.

Edwardian suit An English-inspired man's single- or double-breasted jacket with a four-button (or more) closing. It has a suppressed waist, deep center or side vents, and wide notched lapels. Trousers can be straight or flared.

Greatcoat An English term for a heavy overcoat that sometimes has a belt, is usually double-breasted, and has a collar with a neck closing.

Hourglass suit Men's suit styling which has been the most popular in the United States in the past decade. The jacket features slightly padded shoulders, a fitted waist, and full skirt about the hips.

Blazer

Bomber jacket

Figure 2–4

Jogging suit   Sports-oriented garment worn by men and women. It is usually made of sweatshirt fabric and features a sweatshirt top and pants gathered at the waistline and ankles (Figure 2–6).

Mackinaw or lumberjack   A short, heavy, double-breasted coat usually made of wool plaid.

Mandarin   A coat or jacket adapted from the costume of Chinese mandarins (high officials) during the Chinese Empire. It features a small stand-up collar, kimono

sleeves, side slashes, and an asymmetric closing.

Nehru jacket   A jacket popularized by Nehru, former prime minister of India. It features a straight, boxy cut, straight set-in sleeves, a buttoned front closure, and stiff, separated stand-up collar.

Norfolk   A single-breasted, hip-length, belted jacket with patch pockets and yoke, and box pleats in the front and back. It is worn by both men and women.

Overcoat   A warm, heavy coat worn over

Cape

Chesterfield

Chanel suit

Figure 2–5

Man's suit

Jogging suit

Figure 2–6

other clothing as an outergarment.

Pants coat A woman's casual coat, usually fingertip length, originally intended to be worn over pants. It can be made in a variety of styles and is also known as a car coat.

Pants suit A woman's suit consisting of a jacket or blazer and a coordinating pair of pants. A vest may also be included.

Parka A hooded jacket, often with a fleece lining, used for active sports. The first parkas, made of caribou skin, originated with the Eskimos.

Pea jacket A short single- or double-breasted coat of heavy woolen fabric worn by sailors for warmth. It has also been adapted for street wear as a winter coat.

Poncho A rectangular piece of cloth with no seams and with a hole in the center for the head. It is made in many fabrics, including waterproof materials for rainwear.

Raincoat A water-repellent or waterproof coat worn over clothing for protection from the rain. Many raincoats are highly fashionable and are worn as regular all-weather coats.

Redingote (RED in goht) A French term for adaptations of the English riding coat. It is a simple coat, usually fitted and beltless, and worn with a coordinating dress.

Reefer A single- or double-breasted woman's coat that is princess styled.

Riding jacket A long, single-breasted jacket with slanting pockets. The skirt is flared and has a center vent or two side vents in the back for comfort when the wearer is astride a horse. It is also known as a hacking jacket.

Sack suit A man's suit which is boxy and unfitted, usually with a single rear vent. It is a conservative suit popularized by Brooks Brothers stores.

Safari jacket A jacket, generally of a lightweight fabric, with lapels, four pockets, epaulets, and a belt, adapted from the jacket sportsmen wear on safari (Figure 2–7).

Shawl A wrap originally worn by peasant women. It is a square piece of fabric folded on the diagonal to form a triangle and is often fringed.

Shell A separate warm lining that can be zipped, buttoned, or snapped into a coat.

Ski jacket A lightweight but warm jacket designed for skiers. It is often quilted and made of water-repellent nylon to resist moisture, is interlined with down or polyester fiber for warmth, and has a zipper front and a hidden hood. It is now available in a variety of bright colors (Figure 2–7).

Skirted suit A woman's suit consisting of a blazer or jacket and a coordinating skirt. It is available in numerous styles and a vest may also be included (Figure 2–8).

Slicker A loose, waterproof coat adapted from the fisherman's coat, originally made from an oil-treated fabric. It is now usually made of vinyl.

Smoking jacket A man's lounging jacket intended to worn at home over a shirt and trousers. It usually has a shawl collar and tie belt. In the 1960s French designer Yves Saint Laurent adapted the look for women's evening clothes. American designer Ralph Lauren revitalized the look in the 1980s.

Spencer A short-jacket that was a predecessor of the man's suit jacket. It is cut close to the body and has slim sleeves.

Sport coat A man's or woman's coat, often patterned, worn as a topcoat over casual attire.

Sport jacket A man's jacket, often checked, striped, or plaid, worn over contrasting trousers.

Suit For men, a garment consisting of a jacket, trousers, and sometimes a vest; for women, a suit combining a jacket with a skirt or pants and sometimes a vest (Figure 2–6).

Tail coat A man's formal coat, usually in black or white, featuring long tails in the back.

Topcoat A lightweight overcoat worn by men and women.

Trench coat Adapted from the World War I English officer's coat, it is used now by men and women as a raincoat or sportcoat. It is double-breasted, with a wide belt, military collar, pockets, and epaulets.

Tuxedo or dinner jacket A man's semiformal single- or double-breasted

Safari jacket

Ski jacket

Figure 2–7

evening jacket with a peaked or shawl collar. The tuxedo usually has matching trousers; the dinner jacket, contrasting trousers.

Vest A garment for men, women, or children either woven or knitted, which can be worn with pants or a skirt, or coordinated as part of a suit. It is generally short, stopping at the waist or hips, and sleeveless (Figure 2–8). It can be V-neck or crewneck, buttoned-front, pullover, or buttonless.

Windbreaker A sport jacket with front zipper and elasticized waistband and cuffs. It is usually made of poplin or nylon and has a water-repellent finish.

PANTS

Baggies Women's pants, popularized in the 1970s, which are gathered below the waistband, full through the hips, and tapered to the ankle.

Vest

Skirted suit

Figure 2–8

Fashion Color, Line, and Design

Bell-bottom pants   Men's and women's pants, popular during the 1960s, that are narrow through the hips, then form a wide flare from the knee down. They can be cuffed and can have wide belt loops and pockets.

Clean-front   Men's or women's slacks lacking pleats or gathers below the waistband, giving a non-bulky effect (Figure 2–9).

Continental trouser   A man's trouser with an extended waistband, no belt loops, side adjustments, western or slashed pockets, and moderate- or narrow-tapered leg.

Conventional or conservative trouser   A man's pleated or unpleated trouser with either extended waistband or belt loops, side-slashed pockets, full- to moderate-tapered leg, and with or without cuffs.

Cropped pants   Women's pants with a hemline that ends just above the ankle. (Figure 2–9).

Culottes   Women's short pants that look like a skirt, often with concealing front pleats, originally intended for golfing (Figure 2–10).

Dungarees   Sturdy work pants with curved front pockets, front zipper, and reinforcements at stress points. They are generally made in heavy-duty dungaree twill fabric.

Flared   Pants with legs that flare moderately or fully from the hip.

Gaucho pants   Pants inspired by those of the South American cowboys. The pants have fitted hips, then flare to the middle of the calf at the hem.

Harem pants   Soft, full pants that are gathered above the ankle, often used for lounge wear or evening apparel.

Hip-hugger pants   Pants that sit on the hipbone rather than on the waist. The rise, or distance between the waistband and crotch, is short. The legs can be straight or flared.

Ivy league   Men's trousers with belt loops, side-slashed pockets, full- to moderate-tapered legs, and cuffs.

Jeans   Pants originally made of cotton denim with yokes (western syling), a front zipper, front and back pockets, and straight or flare leg. The "designer jean" fad of the 1970s through '80s, influenced by American designer Calvin Klein, introduced new fabrics, styling, and colors to the jean market.

Jodhpurs   Riding pants that are full and loose from hip to calf, tight-fitting from calf to ankle, and commonly worn tucked inside the wearer's boot.

Jumpsuit   A one-piece garment with or without sleeves, and with straight or flare legs, that is an updated version of the industrial coverall (Figure 2–10). It is made in many styles and fabrics.

Knickers   Shortened form of the term "knickerbockers." Knickers are loose pants for men and women that are gathered below the knee into a snug band. They are also called "plus fours" when they extend 4 inches below the break in the knee. Plus fours were popularized as sportswear in the early twentieth century by the Prince of Wales.

Overalls   Loose pants with a panel that extends over the chest and is held in place by shoulder straps. Overalls originally were made in sturdy fabrics and were worn by farmers and railroad workers. Later they were adapted for children's wear and now they are seen as sportswear.

Pedal pushers   Slim pants that end just below the knee (Figure 2–10). "Toreador pants" are a tighter version and "clam diggers" a looser version. Side vents are often added for ease in movement.

Shorts   Pants that end anywhere from the top of the knee (Bermuda, or walking, shorts) to the top of the thigh (short shorts).

Ski pants   Stretch pants designed for skiers. They may be loose or tight and usually have foot straps to hold them in place under ski boots.

Straight-leg pants   Pants that form a straight line from the hip to the ankle. They may be cuffed or cuffless.

Clean front pants

Cropped pants

Figure 2–9

Culottes

Jumpsuit

Pedal pushers

Figure 2–10

NECKLINES AND COLLARS

Ascot A scarf or tie originally worn at the racetrack in Ascot, England, tied with the wide ends hanging over each other and often held in place by a stickpin.

Backless A neckline with a high front and no back.

Band collar A stand up collar similar to a Chinese collar but without a front slit. It is also known as a Johnny collar.

Bateau (ba TOH) French for "boat." A bateau neckline is a wide neckline close to the neck that curves slightly from points on the shoulder seams (Figure 2–11).

Bertha A capelike collar that extends from the neckline to over the shoulder.

Bib Originally a tiny apron tied around the neck of an infant. It has been adapted to women's dresses and blouses. A bib effect is common on women's tuxedo blouses.

Bow A separate scarf or strip of fabric attached at the neckline and tied in a bow (Figure 2–11).

Buster Brown A high, small, round collar, usually with a contrasting ribbon bow.

Button-down A collar with buttonholes on the points. The points button onto the shirt front. This collar is used on both men's and women's shirts (Figure 2–11).

Chinese A small, stand-up collar slit in the front. It is also called mandarin and was originally part of Chinese native dress.

Choir boy A large collar with points adapted from those that choir boys wear. There is a big, self-tied bow under the collar.

Choker A ribbon, piece of jewelry, scarf, or collar worn tight around the neck.

Chou (shoo) French for "cabbage." A chou is a ribbon or fabric-draped knot resembling a cabbage, that is worn at the neck. It may also be placed at the waistline or on a hat.

Collarless A neckline without a collar. The garment may have lapels.

Convertible A straight-edged collar, usually with points, that may be worn open or closed.

Cowl A soft, bias-cut neckline draped in the front or back of the garment (Figure 2–12). This collar was originally introduced by French designer, Madeleine Vionnet.

Cravat A piece of fabric or a scarf tied around the neck. The cravat was the forerunner of the men's necktie.

Crew A term that comes from the neckline of sweaters worn by rowing crews. It is a round neckline that fits close to the base of the neck (Figure 2–12). Commonly seen on men's and women's sweaters.

Detachable A removable collar.

Dickey A detachable collar or shirtfront that gives the illusion of an underblouse or turtleneck. Dickeys are worn to eliminate bulk under the garment.

Fichu (FISH oo) A collar generally made of a sheer fabric tied in front around the shoulders like a triangular scarf.

Four-in-hand A neckline tied with a slipknot, which allows the end to overlap vertically.

Halter A sleeveless, backless, bodice held by a strap encircling the neck.

High A neckline that is high to the throat.

Jabot (zha BOH) A trimming added to the front of a dress or blouse, originally worn by men (Figure 2–12). It can be ruffled, pleated, embroidered, or lacy.

Keyhole A neckline that is usually round and closed at the throat. Below the neckline there is a teardrop-shaped opening.

Lapel The facing on the front of a garment that folds back across the chest and is attached to the collar.

Military A collar adapted from military uniforms, buttoning high on the neck.

Necktie A band of fabric worn around the neck or under a collar and tied in the front in a knot, bow, or loop.

Notched lapel A lapel with a wide, V-shaped space between it and the collar (Figure 2–12).

Off-the-shoulder A neckline that extends over the shoulder line (Figure 2–13).

Peaked lapel A pointed lapel with a narrow space between it and the collar.

Bateau neckline

Bow

Button-down collar

Figure 2–11

Peter Pan A rounded collar that lies flat (Figure 2–13). It is adapted from the costume worn by Peter Pan in Barrie's play of the same name.

Plunge A neckline or collar that dips low in the front.

Pointed A collar with long or short tapered ends.

Puritan A wide, flat, round collar similar to those worn by the Puritans.

Round or jewel A round neckline, either high or low, or a round collar of any width.

Ruching (ROO shing) Narrow, decorative fabric, pleated and worn at the neck as a collar.

Ruff A high, circular collar that is gathered or pleated. Also known as a pierrot collar, it was adapted from costumes of sixteenth- and seventeenth-century Europe.

Cowl neck

Crew neck

Jabot

Notched lapel

Figure 2–12

Off-the-shoulder neckline

Peter Pan collar

Sailor collar

Figure 2–13

Ruffled   Any type of collar made from ruffles (see "Construction Details").

Sailor   The traditional collar used on the middy blouse. The sailor collar has a square flap back and slants to a V in front. It is often in a contrasting color to the blouse (Figure 2–13).

Scarf   An attached or separate piece of fabric—rectangular, square, or triangular—that is tied around the neck.

Shawl   A collar formed by rolling back the unnotched lapels (Figure 2–14). It is also known as the "bathrobe collar" because it was inspired by the bathrobes of the 1940s.

Shirt   A pointed or rounded collar which is attached to a band that holds the collar stiffly upright. The band, known as the stand, is attached to the shirt.

Slotted   A man's shirt collar that has stays on the underside to keep the collar from curling.

Spread   A man's basic shirt collar with points that are spread apart.

Square   A collar or a neckline that has squared-off corners (Figure 2–14).

Strapless   A dress bodice or blouse that has built-in support and isn't held up by straps (Figure 2–15).

Surplice   A term originally referring to the white vestment worn over the cassock of Roman Catholic and Anglican clergy. It now also refers to a V-neckline formed by wrapping one front half of a garment over the other, then fastening it at the side.

Sweetheart   A neckline that forms the top of a heart in the front (Figure 2–15). It can be high or low. This style is popular in evening wear and wedding attire.

Tab   A man's shirt collar with attached tabs in front that close to hold the points in place.

Turtleneck   A high, snug collar that is turned or rolled over, commonly used on sweaters (Figure 2–15). A mock turtleneck gives the same appearance, but is not turned over.

U-neck   A neckline that forms a U-shape in the front.

Vandyke   A broad, pointed collar with a lace edge that was adapted from those in the portraits painted by Vandyke, a seventeenth-century Flemish painter.

V-neck   A neckline that slants from the shoulder seams to the center front, forming a V.

Windsor tie   A man's necktie tied in a double bowknot with the ends overlapping vertically. This tie necessitates a wider collar spread than most ties. A half-Windsor is not as wide because it is only knotted once.

Wing   A standing collar of stiffened fabric with wing tips. It is often seen on men dressed for formal occasions.

SLEEVES AND CUFFS

Barrel or button cuff   A single shirt cuff that has a button closing. The simplest cuff has one button; more exaggerated styles have four or more buttons.

Bell   A short or long set-in sleeve that flares into a bell shape. The bell starts below the cap or below the **armscye,** which is the name for the opening in the bodice where the sleeve is attached.

Bishop   A long set-in sleeve with a narrow cap that increases in width to the cuff where it is gathered (Figure 2–16).

Cap   A short, kimono sleeve which ends at, or just below, the armhole.

Cape   A sleeve that is a short cape attached at the shoulder. It is open on the underside of the arm.

Convertible cuff   A single cuff with a buttonhole on each side but with only one button. The cuff can be buttoned or worn with links.

Dolman   A long sleeve that curves from a wide armhole to a narrow wrist (Figure 2–16). It is also known as a "batwing sleeve."

Drop shoulder   The shoulder line of a coat, jacket, dress, or blouse that extends over the upper arm (Figure 2–16). A sleeve can be attached.

Elbow length   A sleeve for women's garments that ends at the wearer's elbow.

Shawl collar

Square collar

Figure 2–14

French cuff   A double shirt cuff; that is, one that turns back and fastens with cufflinks.

Kimono   A sleeve adapted from the Japanese kimono that is cut in one piece with the bodice (Figure 2–17). It has a high underarm and a slight curve over the shoulder. A gusset is often added for ease of movement when the kimono sleeve is long.

Lantern   A set-in sleeve which flares from the shoulder to, or near, the elbow, where there is a seam. Below that point, the sleeve tapers into the arm. The shape resembles a Chinese lantern.

Leg-of-mutton   A long, set-in sleeve popularized by the Gibson Girl look of the 1890s. The sleeve is gathered for fullness over the shoulder and upper arm, but fits tightly below the elbow.

Strapless dress

Sweetheart neckline

Turtleneck

Figure 2–15

Bishop sleeve   *Dolman sleeve*   *Drop shoulder*

Figure 2–16

Melon A short, full sleeve, usually with gores (see "Construction Details") to give a puffed shape.

Petal A set-in sleeve that appears to wrap around the arm, with one section overlapping another, forming a petaled effect.

Puff A set-in sleeve that is gathered at the shoulder for fullness. The short version looks like a full melon sleeve. The longer version is full to the wrist, where it is gathered in a tight cuff.

Push-up A close-fitting sleeve that is set-in or raglan and worn pushed up to, or above, the elbow rather than at its full length. This sleeve is common in women's sportswear.

Raglan A woman's sleeve that is cut to extend to the neckline and thus includes the garment's shoulder (Figure 2–17). The raglan forms a rounded, narrow shoulder line.

Ribbed cuff A knitted cuff that has raised ridges or wales and is snug-fitting.

Roll-up A straight, casual, set-in sleeve that is hemmed and then rolled to the desired length, usually just above the elbow (Figure 2–17).

Saddle shoulder Variation of the raglan sleeve. The saddle shoulder is a square cut from the neck across the shoulder.

Set-in Any sleeve that is sewn or set into a regular armhole. The armhole can be high or low, and the sleeve can be long or short, straight or full.

Shirt A long, set-in sleeve that is gathered, although it isn't full, into either a button, a convertible, or a French cuff.

Sleeveless A garment with no sleeves.

Suit A long, straight, tapered set-in sleeve, usually with a dart at the elbow for smooth fit.

Three-quarter length A sleeve which ends between the wearer's elbow and wrist.

Wing A set-in sleeve which is fully gathered and stiffly stands away from the bodice. This sleeve is commonly seen on pinafores. It is also known as a "butterfly sleeve."

CONSTRUCTION DETAILS

Appliqué (ap luh KAY) A piece of fabric in a decorative shape that is sewn or glued to another fabric or garment.

Basting A temporary row of hand or machine stitching used to hold garment sections together during clothing construction. Basting stitches are longer than normal machine stitches.

Beading Applying beads to a garment whether by hand or machine. Beading adds a "glittery" appearance to garments. American designer Bob Mackie has popularized this look with cylinder-shaped bugle beads.

Belted Any garment with a belt.

Bias The true bias on cloth is a 45-degree angle to the warp (lengthwise threads). Garments cut on the bias drape easily, because the bias stretches. Bias-cut fabric is also used when cling is desired.

Binding Single- or double-fold bias tape, braid, or lace used to finish the raw edges or seams on a garment. It may be sewn or ironed onto the garment.

Bodice The portion of the garment which extends from the neckline to the waistline.

Braid A trimming or binding which may be woven, tubular, or plaited.

Button A fastening or ornament on a garment, usually in the shape of a disk or knob. Buttons may be fundamental or ornamental. They may be applied by sewing through the center of the button or by sewing through a shank or stem on the button's underside. A button used for a fastening closes through a buttonhole slit or loop. Buttons are made in many materials including bone, leather, metal, plastic, shell, and wood. Some are covered in fabric.

Circular Any garment or part of a garment that is cut in a round shape (also includes semicircular).

Cording A decoration used on apparel made by running a thin cord through a bias strip of fabric and stitching it to a garment at an edge or seam. It can also be put in a tuck.

Kimono sleeve

Raglan sleeve

Roll-up sleeve

Figure 2–17

Cut-and-sewn Garments that are made from different parts that are cut out and sewn together (as opposed to knitted garments).

Dart A tuck that is stitched along a line tapering to a point. Darts are used to shape a garment and create a smoother fit.

Embroidery Decorative needlework applied by hand or machine.

Epaulet An ornament, often of braid, worn on the shoulders of a garment. It was originally worn on military uniforms. In sportswear, an epaulet is a fabric tab sewn onto the shoulders.

Eyelet A small hole finished with a buttonhole stitch. It can be an embroidery decoration or a hole for lacing.

Facing A piece of fabric that is either an extension of, or a separate piece sewn into, the inside edge of a garment to finish, decorate, or support it.

Findings Functional, not ornamental, elements of a garment such as linings, facings, buttons, elastic, hooks and eyes, zippers, and snaps.

Fitted A garment that lies close to the body.

Flounce A wide, decorative ruffle.

Fly front A garment closure that is an overlapping fold of cloth hiding a zipper or other fastenings.

Fringe A hanging trim made from threads or cords.

Frog Decorative loop fastening made of braid or cording.

Full fashioned A shaped knitted garment made on a flat knitting machine by increasing and decreasing stitches. The term is often used for sweaters.

Gathering Pulling cloth along a thread to create small folds or puckers to give controlled fullness in a section of a garment.

Gimp A ribbon-like trim, often with wire or cord stiffening in the core.

Godet (goh DAY) A triangular insert added to a garment for flare, usually near the hem).

Gore A shaped panel added to a dress, shirt, or coat for fullness. It is also an elastic panel added to a shoe for ease in putting on and removing the shoe.

Grain The direction in which the warp yarns and the weft yarns are woven in fabric. The warp yarns make up the lengthwise grain, and the weft yarns make up the crosswise grain.

Gusset A shaped piece of material, often triangular, sewn into a garment (usually under the arm) for extra room and strength. It is common in long kimono sleeves.

Hem The raw edge of a garment, usually the bottom edge, which is folded back and stitched. It may be straight, curved, rolled, faced, bound, or piped.

Hook and eye A closure consisting of a curved piece of metal wire (the hook) that catches a round or straight loop (the eye). The eye may be made of thread or metal.

Interfacing Fabric cut the same as the facing and sewn between the facing and the garment for additional support. It may be woven, nonwoven, fusible, or nonfusible.

Interlining Fabric cut the same as the lining and sewn between the lining and the garment for warmth.

Lace Fabric that is woven together in an open design. It may be made of silk, linen, cotton, or polyester.

Lacing A cord or ribbon that is used for closing shoes and some garments. Two ends of the lacing loop through eyelets or hooks, cross each other, and then loop again until the item is fastened.

Lining Fabric which is cut, shaped, sewn together, and then attached to the inside of a garment. It serves as a finishing touch to a garment's interior and aids the wearer in slipping the garment on and off.

Overcasting A stitching technique used to finish off seams or in embroidery. It can be machine- or hand-stitched.

Padding A soft material used to thicken certain parts of a garment such as the shoulders in a jacket or suit. It is also used to give contour in the cups of brassieres.

Paillette (PY yet) A large sequin-like disk sewn onto fabric or a garment for decoration.

Picot (PEE koh)   A small loop of thread used in a series as an edging on ribbon, lace, or a garment.

Pinking   Cutting the edge of a fabric or garment in a sawtooth pattern. It is used for decoration and as a seam finish to prevent raveling.

Piping   A piece of fabric, cord, or braid used as trim on the edge or seam of a garment.

Placket   A finished slit in a garment for ease in putting it on and removing it.

Pleats   Folds of fabric that are usually pressed or stitched in place to add fullness to a garment. There are many different kinds of pleats (Figure 2–18):

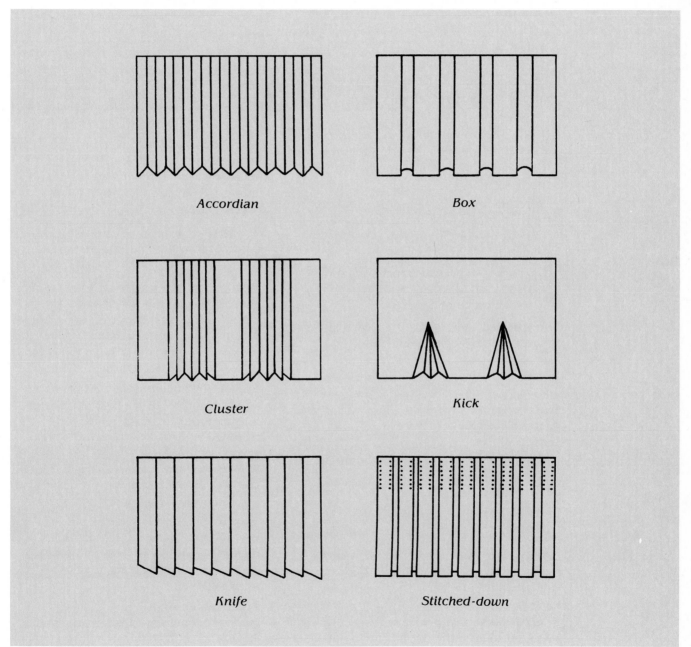

Accordian

Box

Cluster

Kick

Knife

Stitched-down

Figure 2–18
Types of pleating.

Accordian   Thin, even pleats, one folded over another like the bellows of an accordian.

Box   Two knife pleats folded to face each other on the wrong side of the garment.

Cartridge   Pleats with a rounded top, giving a tubular effect.

Cluster   A grouping of several types of soft pleats, excluding knife pleats.

Inverted   Two knife pleats folded away from each other on the wrong side of the garment.

Kick   Similar to an inverted pleat, a kick pleat is usually placed low on a straight garment to give extra room for movement.

Knife   Narrow pleats all turned in the same direction, usually right to left, around the body. They are also known as side pleats.

Stitched-down   Pleats which have been sewn from the waist to the hip on either the right side or the wrong side for a smooth fit over the hipline.

Sunburst   Pleats which increase in width from the top of the pleat to the bottom for a fan or sunburst effect.

Unpressed   Pleats that are folded but are neither pressed nor stitched down.

Pocket   A pouchlike piece of fabric sewn into or onto a garment for decoration or for carrying small articles. There are several kinds of pockets:

Patch pocket   Pocket stitched onto the face of a garment.

Set-in pocket   Pocket inside a special opening on a garment.

Pocket set into a seam   Pocket that has an opening on the seam with the pouch stitched behind it.

Slash pocket   A pocket on the inside of the garment with a slashed and flapped opening on the outside. There are three types of slash pockets—welt, bound, and flap.

Quilting   Sewing soft padding between two layers of fabric. It is usually done in crossed lines or in a pattern.

Reversible   A fabric or garment which can be used on either side.

Ribbon   Narrow strips of woven fabric with finished selvages, often tied, that are used for trimming, fastening, or decorating.

Rickrack   A decorative woven trim that forms a sawtooth pattern.

Ruche (roosh)   A pleated or frilled piece of lace, ribbon, or decorative fabric used as trimming.

Ruffle   A narrow, gathered, pleated piece of fabric used as a trim (Figure 2–19).

Seam   The line formed when two pieces of fabric are sewn or joined together to form parts of a garment. Seams can be sewn by hand or by machine. There are many different types of seams:

Corded   A plain seam with a strip of cording sewn into it on the right side of the garment, similar to the piped seam.

Flat fell   A plain seam used for men's shirts, pajamas, and sportswear. After a plain seam is sewn with the wrong sides together, one seam allowance is trimmed, the other is folded over it, and they are topstitched to the garment.

French   A double seam used primarily on sheer fabrics. A plain seam is stitched on the right side of the fabric and trimmed and pressed, then the fabric is turned right sides together, and a second seam is made, enclosing the raw edges of the first.

Lapped   A seam used on yokes and gussets. The seam allowance of the added part (yoke or gusset) is folded under. It is then placed with right sides up over the seam allowance of the main piece and sewn together.

Piped   A decorative seam that has a piece of piping sewn between the seam edges on the right side of a garment. The piping is usually contrasting.

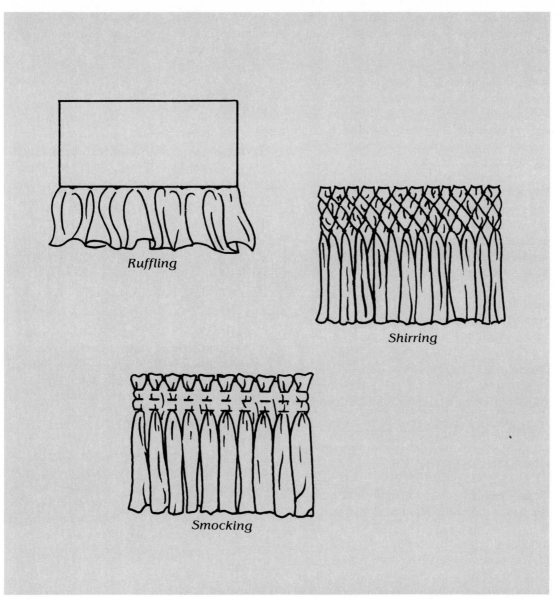

Figure 2–19
Stitching effects.

Plain   The most common seam, used to join the parts of a garment. The edges of the garment sections to be joined are lined up, right sides of fabric together, then the seam is stitched on the wrong side and pressed open.

Saddle stitching   A decorative, hand-topstitched seam, often done on leather with contrasting thread.

Slot   A decorative seam with a contrasting piece of fabric showing through. The seam allowances from the two edges to be joined are folded under to form tucks. The contrasting piece of fabric is inserted under the tucks, and the tucks are stitched to it.

Topstitched   A plain seam which has a row of hand stitching or machine stitching on the right side. A double topstitched seam has a row of stitching on both sides of the plain seam.

Welt   A seam used for sportswear and heavy fabrics. A plain seam is stitched with the right sides together, then pressed open. One seam allowance is trimmed, and the other is folded over it and stitched to the garment.

Selvage   The finished "self-edge" which runs lengthwise, or warpwise, on both edges of woven fabric. The selvage keeps the cloth straight and even, and prevents it from raveling. Selvage also refers to the finished edge on knitted cloth.

Semi-fitted   A garment that does not precisely follow the contour of the body, but yet is slightly fitted.

Sequin   Plastic discs which are sewn onto garments for a glittering effect. They are available in a variety of sizes and colors.

Shirring   A series of parallel rows of running stitches that are drawn together to form gathers (Figure 2–19).

Single-breasted   A garment with one row of buttons down the front as the closure.

Smocking   Rows of decorative stitching in a honeycomb pattern that hold fullness in place evenly on a garment (Figure 2–19). It is very popular in little girls' garments.

Snaps   A two-piece circular metal or fabric-covered closure used on garment sections where there is light stress. One piece has a small ball in the center that is pressed into a hole on the other piece.

Tiers   Rows of ruffles or flounces on a garment layered one on top of another.

Trapunto   A type of quilting with a raised design. Each part of the pattern is outlined with stitches and padded separately.

Tuck   A small fold that is stitched in place. It is used to hold fullness, to shorten, to shape, or to decorate. A pin tuck is a very small tuck, usually used in a series for decoration.

Underlining   A lightweight fabric which is cut, shaped, and sewn to the wrong side of a garment before final construction. Used as a support to the fabric and design line, as well as reinforcement to the seams.

Yoke   A separate section of fabric set into a garment, usually to support pleats or gathers. The yoke in a bodice extends from the shoulders to a seam right above the bustline. A shirt may have a yoke in the back only or, as in a Western-styled shirt, in both the front and back. Pants and skirts can have a yoke from the waistband to the hipline.

Zipper   A closure consisting of a sliding tab on a track of metal teeth or polyester coil. A zipper is usually set in a placket.

Projects

1. From current newspapers and fashion magazines, find illustrations of five different styles in each of the categories listed below. Include samples of clothing for men, women, and children. Label the illustrations using the terms in this chapter and mount the illustrations in your notebook.
   a. dresses and skirts
   b. jackets, coats, and vests
   c. blouses and shirts
   d. pants
   e. collars and necklines
   f. sleeves

2. From current newspapers and fashion magazines, find illustrations of ten different garments. Write a description of each garment's design details, using the terminology in this chapter. The ten garments selected should reflect women's, men's, and children's fashions.

3
Design Lines and Principles

In order to understand fashion design, you must first be familiar with the basic principles involved. This understanding can make the difference between a successful design and a failure.

By applying the basic principles and making the correct use of line, the designer can conceive a garment which is not only creative, but also marketable. This is extremely important to the designer, as designs are considered successful only when they sell to the public.

LINES

The simplest design form is the line (Figure 3–1). Lines can be straight, curved, broken, or bent to form angles. They can be thick or thin. They can be placed vertically, horizontally, or diagonally. Lines can also be used in designs to create optical illusions. Line usage in a garment pertains both to the lines printed on the fabric as well as to the structural lines within the garment including pleats, pockets, seams, topstitching, and gathers.

Understanding line usage is extremely important when designing a garment. For example, garments consisting only of straight lines would be too harsh, while a careful balance of straight and curved lines would create a marketable design.

Just as colors are seen subjectively, so are lines. Vertical lines denote strength and conservatism. They slim and add height to the wearer. Horizontal lines denote calmness. This may be because they appear to be lying down or because still water or flat land has a horizontal line. Horizontal lines also add width to the wearer. Diagonal lines denote action by leading the eye through the garment. Zig-zag lines add excitement, yet are sometimes confusing to the eye. Curved lines and spirals create movement. Thick lines are bold, while thin ones are delicate. The S-shaped curve, or ogee (OH jee), is called the line of beauty. Apparel designed with S curves is flattering to the wearer and appealing to the eye.

Correct use of line leads the eye through the garment smoothly, rather than haphazardly. Knowledge of lines is also useful for camouflaging the wearer's figure problems. Petite women, as well as large women, often use vertical lines to create the optical illusion of height and slimness. On the other hand, women who want to look shorter or heavier may do so with the help of horizontal lines.

Silhouette

Silhouette is the form of the garment. The importance of silhouette lies in the fact that the visual shape of the body is achieved by the garment that is worn. Throughout history, silhouettes have been consistently repeated (see Chapter 6).

The **tubular silhouette**—straight up and down—is popular when people are concerned with dieting and physical fitness, as during the 1920s and 1980s. The **bell silhouette,** which emphasizes the bustline and hips, is popular when women are less

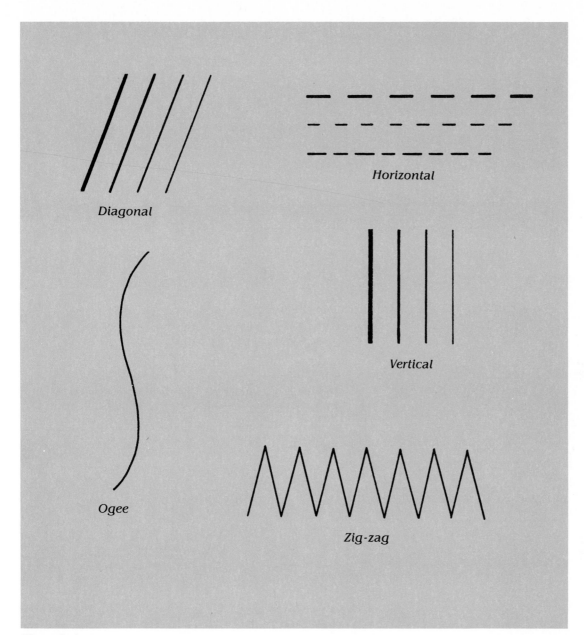

Figure 3–1
Types of lines.

conscious of fitness and when more weight is fashionable, as in the Victorian era and during the 1950s. Designers regularly adapt these silhouettes, exaggerating various body parts to create interest and introduce fashion trends. They add interest to the silhouette with padding, fabric, draping, and construction lines (Figure 3—2).

Emphasis on the shoulders as a fashion trend was demonstrated by American designer, Norma Kamali, in her early 1980s designs featuring a well-padded, exaggerated shoulder area.

DESIGN PRINCIPLES

The development of a successful design also depends on the understanding of basic design principles, including proportion, balance, emphasis, rhythm, and harmony. Although each principle is a separate entity,

Tubular silhouette

Bell silhouette

Figure 3–2
The tubular silhouette (left) is a straight form; the bell silhouette emphasizes the hips and the bustline.

Fashion Color, Line, and Design

combining them successfully produces an appealing garment.

Proportion

All segments of a garment must be in proportion to each other, as well as in proportion to the size of the wearer. Seasonal fashion changes may affect proportion. The style of a short jacket and longer skirt one season may shift the proportional balance the next season with designers featuring a longer jacket with shorter skirts.

Proportion in details in a garment must be consistent to be effective. For example, the size of the collar should reflect the size of the cuffs, buttons, sleeves, etc. Small detailing, such as dainty tucks, are usually accompanied by narrow cuffs, a narrow collar, and small buttons. In menswear, the width of collars will reflect a proportional change in the width of neckties.

Proportion of garments also applies to the size of the wearer. Smaller details and accessories would lend themselves to a petite wearer, but would be overpowered by a larger individual. A large, bold print would be appropriate on a larger person but would "drown" a petite individual. Proportion may also follow natural body divisions or break away and create new divisions within the garment (Figure 3—3).

Balance

Balance in a garment is determined by visually dividing the garment straight down the center. If one side mirrors the other, formal, or symmetrical, balance has been achieved (Figure 3—4). Formal balance denotes conservatism and is common in professional clothing.

If the line down the center of the garment leaves one side different from the other, informal, or asymmetrical, balance has been achieved (Figure 3—4). Informal balance is especially popular in evening wear, as it is more dramatic and glamorous.

Emphasis

The emphasis, or the focal point, of the garment is the area that first attracts the viewer's eye (Figure 3—5). Emphasis adds interest to the garment and may be created by the use of color, design lines, detailing, or accessories.

Wearers should avoid creating a focal point in an area of the body to which they do not want to draw attention. Many garments are designed with the emphasis near the collar area to call attention to the wearer's face.

Rhythm

Rhythm is the repeating of lines, colors, trimmings, or details to create a pattern by which the eye can flow through the garment. If the repetition is random, it is known as unequal rhythm, which adds interest to the garment. Equal rhythm occurs when line, color, or detail are spaced at equidistant intervals. Designers must take care that this form of repetition does not become boring.

Graduated rhythm is achieved when portions of the design are gradually decreased or increased through their repetition.

Harmony

Harmony, or unity, is created when all elements of a design come together in a pleasing harmonious effect. It is a critical factor in producing a marketable design. A garment may undergo numerous design changes before achieving harmony.

It is important to note that while each design line and principle is important, it is the combination of lines and principles that creates a fashion design.

Figure 3–3
The garment shown on the left follows natural body divisions. The garment on the right creates new body divisions within the garment.

Figure 3–4
Formal or symmetrical balance is achieved in the suit on the left. The gown on the right has achieved informal or asymmetrical balance.

Figure 3—5
This model is wearing a scarf for emphasis.

Projects

1. From current newspapers or fashion magazines, find one example of each of the following design lines and principles:
   a. vertical lines
   b. horizontal lines
   c. diagonal lines
   d. curved lines
   e. proportion following natural body divisions
   f. proportion differing from natural body divisions
   g. formal balance
   h. informal balance
   i. emphasis
   j. equal rhythm
   k. graduated rhythm
   l. harmony

2. From current newspapers or fashion magazines, find three examples of garments that you find interesting. Analyze the reasons that these garments appeal to you. Then find three examples of garments that you feel are boring and analyze the reasons that they do not appeal to you.

4
Fashion Drawing

Many jobs in the fashion industry require drawing ability. While it's true that buyers, fashion coordinators, or stylists are neither designers nor illustrators, individuals who can translate fashion concepts into drawings of garments or accessories will more capably fill these positions. A drawing is always clearer than a written description. Designers and illustrators usually spend years studying anatomy and drawing technique to make fashion drawings of today's exceptional quality.

If you're planning a career in the fashion design industry, you'll need to know about fashion drawing. Since your drawings will be used as memory jogs to help write reports or as thumbnail sketches to accompany reports, they should be simple and clear. It will also be helpful to perfect some basic figure poses that can be adapted to whatever fashions you see.

BASIC FIGURE DRAWING

Anyone can learn to draw a basic fashion figure. First, anatomical proportions must be understood. The average person stands 7½ heads high. This means that the distance from head to toe is 7½ times the length of the head. On a female with a 7½-head average figure, the bust would be at 2 heads, the waist at 3, the knees at 5½, and the ankles at 7.

For fashion drawing, an 8½-head figure is generally used. This figure is called a **croquis** (kroh kee) and is an excellent starting tool for beginners (Figures 4–1 and 4–2). Designers use this basic figure to communicate concepts to pattern makers. In magazine or newspaper sketches, however, fashion figures are often exaggerated beyond 8½ heads to 9½ or 10½, since the emphasis is on the line of the clothing rather than on perfect proportion.

Before starting to draw, remember that every figure must be balanced. A balance line is a straight line running down from the pit of the neck through the body to the foot supporting the weight (Figure 4–3). If the weight is equally distributed on both feet, the balance line will center between them (Figure 4–3). Three-quarters, side, and back views are often more suitable than full-front views. Look through fashion magazines for recurring poses.

Clothing is designed for the body in movement. Thus, action sketches are more realistic than stills and add more interest. Body action is indicated by either changing the height of shoulders or hips or altering arm and leg positions (Figure 4–3). Don't exaggerate positions, however, or the emphasis moves from the clothes, where it belongs, to the figure. Also, bear in mind the flexible joints where movement occurs— shoulders, elbows, wrists, waist, hip sockets, knees, and ankles.

Combining a stick and oval figure is a good starting point for simple fashion drawings (Figure 4–4). The first figure you'll draw is full-front with the weight on the left foot, hands on hips. Draw the 8½-

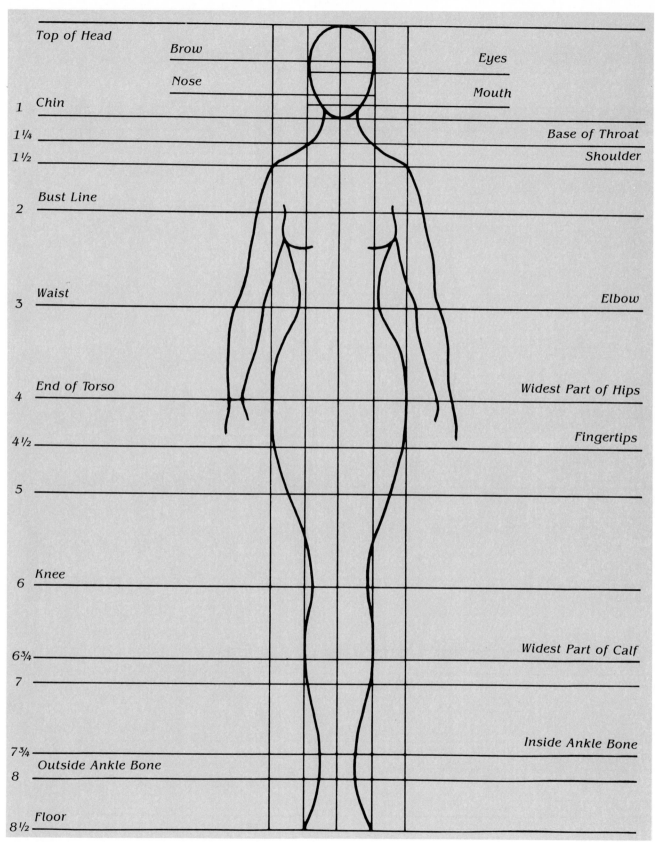

Top of Head

Brow

Eyes

Nose

Mouth

1 Chin

1¼ Base of Throat

1½ Shoulder

Bust Line

2

3 Waist Elbow

4 End of Torso Widest Part of Hips

4½ Fingertips

5

6 Knee

6¾ Widest Part of Calf

7

7¾ Inside Ankle Bone

Outside Ankle Bone

8

8½ Floor

Figure 4–1
This 8½-head length female croquis is a useful tool in fashion drawing.

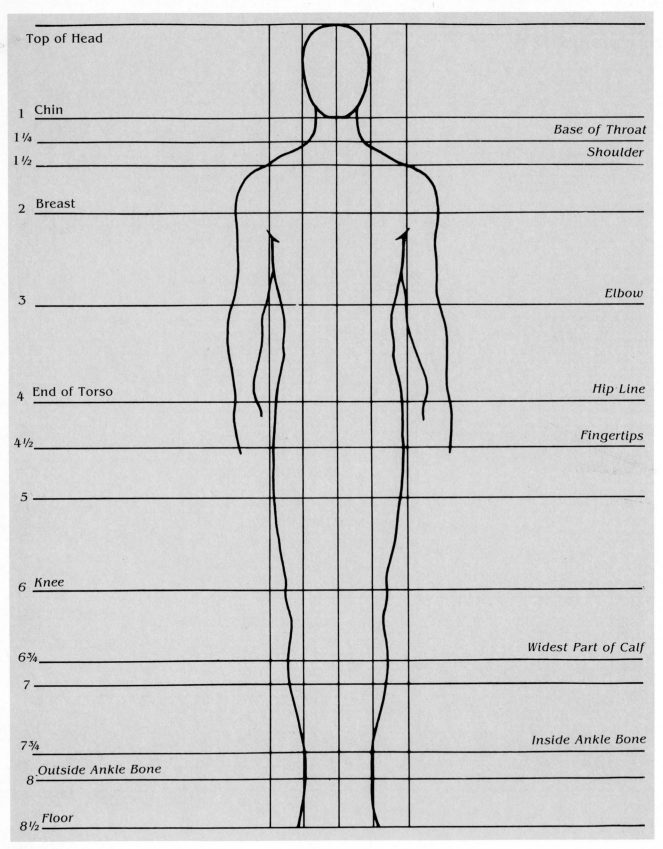

Top of Head

1 Chin

Base of Throat

1¼

Shoulder

1½

2 Breast

3

Elbow

4 End of Torso

Hip Line

4½

Fingertips

5

6 Knee

Widest Part of Calf

6¾

7

7¾

Inside Ankle Bone

Outside Ankle Bone

8

8½ Floor

Figure 4–2
An 8½-head length male croquis.

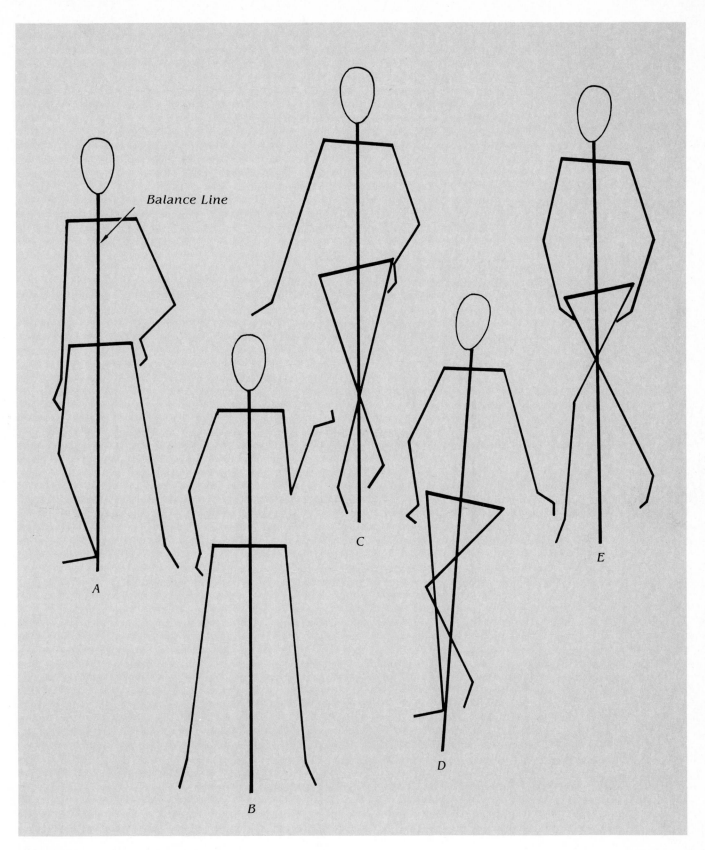

Balance Line

A

B

C

D

E

Figure 4–3
The balance line runs from the neck through the body to the foot.

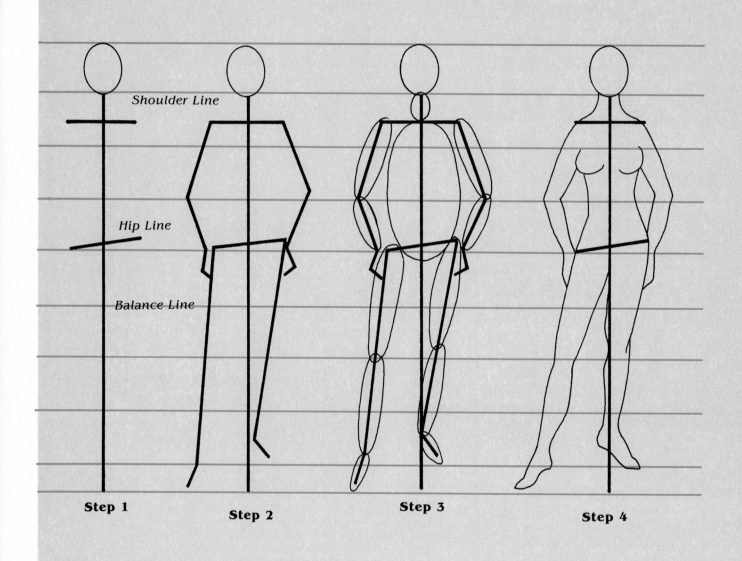

Shoulder Line

Hip Line

Balance Line

Step 1

Step 2

Step 3

Step 4

Figure 4–4
The steps on the left are used to draw a full-front fashion figure. The steps on the right are used to draw a three-quarters pose fashion figure.

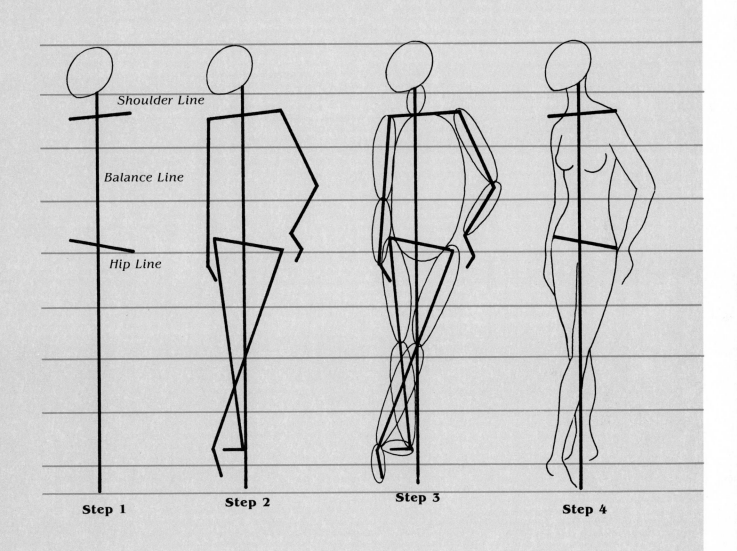

Shoulder Line

Balance Line

Hip Line

Step 1   Step 2   Step 3   Step 4

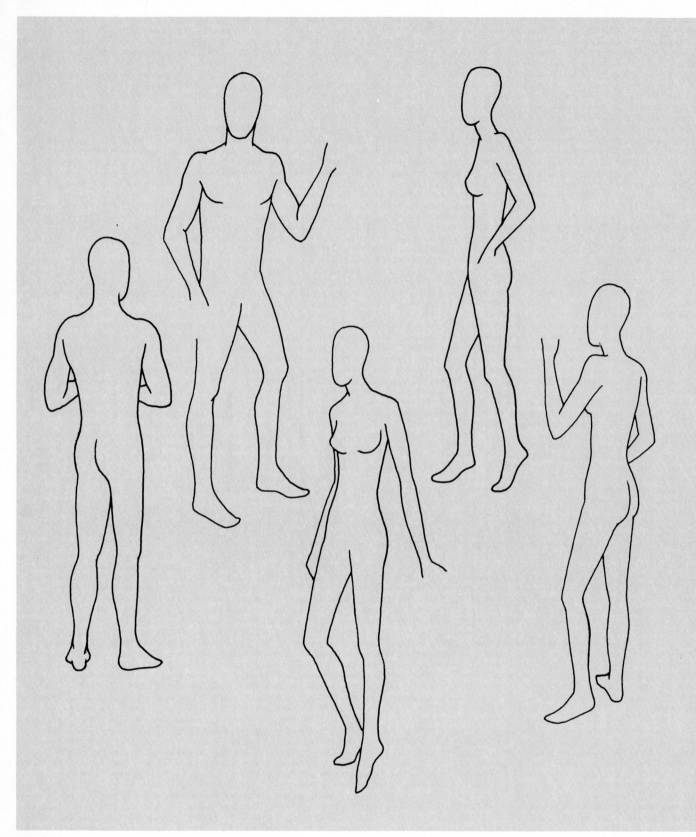

Figure 4–5
Various poses can be used when drawing fashion figures.

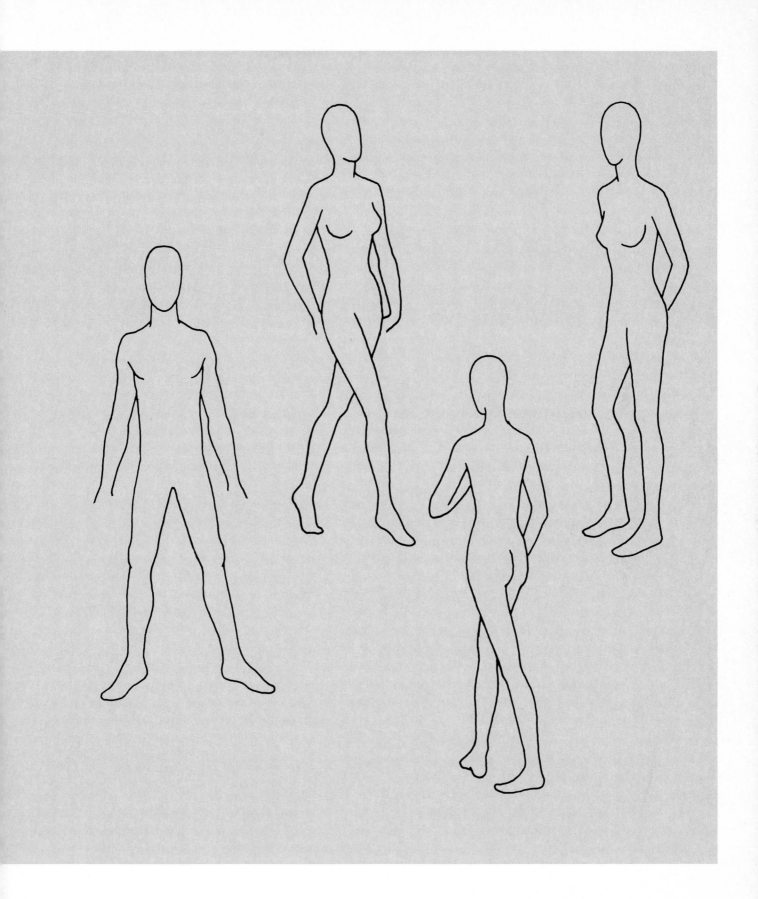

head grid for initial drawings to ensure correct proportions, then follow these steps:

1. Draw the head, balance line, shoulder line, and hip line, as shown in Figure (4–4).
2. Draw the arm and leg lines.
3. Add ovals for body shape.
4. Round out the body silhouette by connecting and trimming the ovals. Figure (4–5) shows a variety of poses. Practice the steps above until you can draw a realistic figure in several poses, visualizing the ovals before drawing them.

DRAWING CLOTHING

After you have mastered figure proportions and basic fashion poses, you can move on to drawing clothing. Keep the figure simple, using a few lines as necessary. Apparel details should be accurate, and sketches should show the movement of the clothing on the body.

Make your drawing three dimensional and have the clothing curve around it. Don't draw flat paper dolls. Keep in mind there will be folds made by the action of the body, the flow of the fabric, the design of the garment—pleats or gathers, for example—or a combination of all three types of folds (Figure 4–6).

You need to understand textiles, or the "feel" of the fabric, in order to draw garments accurately. This is because texture influences how a garment looks. Fabrics of lighter texture fall more fluidly from the shoulders and cling to the body, while heavier fabrics hamper drapability and add bulk to the garment (Figure 4–7). Notes at the side of a sketch indicating fabric characteristics would be helpful, or you might pin a swatch of the fabric to the sketch.

POSE AND CLOTHING RELATIONSHIP

The figure pose and the garment style should be in harmony with each other. For example, active sportswear would look better on a figure showing movement, while an inactive figure would better display a couture evening design. Study fashion magazines and newspaper fashion advertisements to stay abreast of popular poses and illustrative styles. Fashion illustration styles change just as fashions do. Illustrative figures are exaggerations, since the emphasis is not on accuracy of detail but on eye appeal. Thus, proportions may change with clothing styles.

Establish a portfolio of figures to work with. You could carry it with you, or carry predrawn figures inside a notebook. Then when you need a fashion sketch, you can impose the clothing over the predrawn figures.

FASHION DRAWING AND CUSTOMER IMAGE

The type of figure and pose for a fashion drawing should reflect the customer. Customers want a certain "look" that depends on their age, body shape, and body size. Although age may be a factor, the fashion image comes first—and sophistication and style is what customers look for today.

Body Size

There are several figure types that a fashion illustrator must appeal to. The misses size customer is a well-proportioned woman of average height. The petite misses size is shorter, but still well-proportioned. The junior size has small proportions, is shorter waisted, and is generally shorter than the misses customer. Now there is a combined misses/junior size. Further types include the woman's size figure, which is larger, average in height, and mature. The half-size figure is short, full, and has a short back waist length.

Each figure type has a general age range. Juniors are generally in their teens or early twenties, misses are in their mid-twenties or early thirties, and half size and women's sizes are out of their thirties and older.

Figure 4–6
These fashion sketches illustrate movement of clothing on the body.

Figure 4–7
The dress on the left is made of a light, textured fabric and falls fluidly. The outfit on the right consists of heavier fabric, which adds bulkiness.

Color and Texture

Color is an important aspect of customer image. It is the first apparent selling point. Lighter colored fabrics reflect light and will make the wearer's body seem larger. Darker colors will have the opposite effect.

Solid-colored fabrics lend themselves to garments that are intricately designed. This is because the detailing will be more evident without patterns. Intricate designs also do better in lighter weight fabrics since the heavier fabrics add bulk to details, such as tucking, gathering, and smocking.

Some fabrics typify certain apparel categories. Lustrous, metallic fabrics are dressy, while stretch knits are popular for active wear. Wools are typical for suits and expensive sports wear. Cottons are appropriate for many categories of apparel ranging from men's shirts to children's wear.[1]

At some time in your career, taking a fashion drawing course would be beneficial, as would a course in textiles and clothing construction. But until then, the techniques described here should enable you to see and reproduce fashion lines intelligently. Your knowledge of color, line, and design principles, combined with basic fashion drawing, should enable you to take accurate notes and write well-prepared reports.

Projects

1. Go through a fashion magazine or newspaper ads and find ten different poses. With tracing paper overlays, put in the balance line, shoulder line, and hip line.
2. Make a portfolio of twenty different fashion poses.
3. Find ten fashion photographs showing the entire figure. Do a fashion sketch of each.
4. Collect ten fashion illustrations from magazines and newspapers. Overlay them with tracing paper and measure their porportions. Discuss the results.

5. Design an outfit suitable for each of the following figure types and age ranges. Complete each design in color.
   a. tall figure
   b. misses petite
   c. junior petite
   d. misses
   e. junior
   f. half-size
   g. women's
   h. slender figure
   i. stout figure

5

History of Costume

Men and women have been wearing clothing since prehistoric times. Fashion is often a reflection of historical and cultural events. This chapter will introduce you to the costume changes and trends from ancient Egypt to the 1980s.

Throughout the ages clothing has been worn for numerous reasons:

- protection—from injury and from the elements
- modesty—the degree of modesty differing in various cultures
- adornment—wearing jewelry, beads, or other embellishments
- status—to show wealth and social standing
- belonging—evidence you belong to a group, such as tribal wear or Scottish tartans representing clans
- sexual attraction—wearing a garment to attract the opposite sex

Three silhouettes have been repeated in women's fashions throughout history—back interest, tubular, and the bell (Figure 5–1).

The back interest silhouette has the main focus of the garment on the back, such as when the bustle was popular.

The tubular silhouette is straight up and down at the sides, camouflaging the female figure and giving the body a masculine appearance. Its popularity increases during times when women have a strong social position, such as in ancient Egypt, the flappers of the 1920s, during World War II, and in the 1980s with the women's movement.

The bell silhouette emphasizes the curves of the female body and is popular in times when women are at their weakest in society. Examples of this silhouette are Victorian styles, the dresses of the Southern Belles before the U.S. Civil War, and the poodle skirt of the 1950s.

Many factors influence what we wear. An area's customs often dictate what is deemed acceptable. Laws play a role by determining what is legally allowed. Technology plays its part in the new methods of construction and new fabrics that are continuously being developed. Economic developments are also important in determining what fabrics, quality, styling, and number of garments a consumer may purchase. Harris, Upham, and Company charted women's hemlines in relation to the Dow Jones Industrial Average. An interesting theory was developed showing a direct correlation between fashion and the economy: As the stock market went up, hemlines also rose; as the market fell, hemlines followed suit. Reference groups are important since people dress like their peers to be accepted. Current events also influence fashion today. As First Lady, Nancy Reagan has contributed to the fashion industry, as did Jacqueline Kennedy in the 1960s. Great Britain's Princess Diana's sense of style has also influenced fashion in the 1980s. (These contributions will be discussed later in the chapter, under "Twentieth Century.")

During the twentieth century, many fashions have been inspired by entertainers, such as actors and actresses, singers, and

Back interest

Tubular silhouette

Bell silhouette

Figure 5–1
These three silhouettes have been repeated in women's fashion throughout history. Each silhouette places emphasis on a different area of the body.

movie stars. Rock videos have promoted the fashion influences of such singers as Michael Jackson, Madonna, Cyndi Lauper, and Boy George. Among the actresses who have influenced fashion are Jean Harlow (1930s), Joan Crawford (1940s), Marilyn Monroe (1950s), Mia Farrow (1960s), and Diane Keaton (1970s).

Movies have been extremely influential on the fashion industry. The Russian influence of *Dr. Zhivago,* the disco look of *Saturday Night Fever,* the popularity of Western wear caused by *Urban Cowboy,* the layering concept of *Annie Hall,* and the futuristic costumes of *Star Wars* are just a few examples that illustrate how movies have affected fashions.

To help you understand the evolution of costume, this chapter will follow a chronological sequence.

EGYPTIANS: 2800 B.C. TO 300 B.C.

Located in the rich and fertile Nile Valley, the Egyptians practiced a religion based on a belief in the afterlife and a worship of the sun. The sun's influence is reflected through their garments in the form of sunburst pleating and through their jewelry in the form of sun's rays.

The Egyptians regarded their bodies as temples for the soul. They continuously groomed themselves and showed their well-maintained bodies through sheer, form-fitting garments. They removed the hair from the entire body with pumice stones and wore wigs. They used heavy makeup on their eyes, which were considered mirrors to the soul. They lined their eyes with black kohl for cosmetic reasons as well as for protection against the sun's rays (as football players do today).

Egyptian men wore a loincloth known as a **shenti.** It was held in place by a belt. The shenti was often knee-length and shaped in a triangle to reflect the architecture of the pyramids (Figure 5–2).

Linen and woven vegetable fibers were common fabrics. Women wore a transparent linen gown called a **kalasiris** (kah lah SY ris), to exhibit their well-groomed bodies. Pleating was common in the kalasiris, which was usually held in place by a large bejeweled collar at the throat (Figure 5–2).

CRETANS: 2500 B.C. TO 1100 B.C.

The Cretan civilization, located on the island of Crete, was quite advanced. By 2000 B.C., the Cretans had invented a system of written communication. They were also the first people to have central heating and plumbing in their homes.

The Cretans were vain and very proud of their bodies. The women were considered the best-dressed women of the known world. Their vanity was so great that they would sew their own garments to prevent others from duplicating them.

The people were also very proud of their small waistlines (twelve inches maximum) which were achieved by soldering belts on male and female children at age six. Thus began the bell silhouette (Figure 5–3).

Located on the main trade routes of the Mediterranean, the Cretans influenced many of the cultures that surrounded them. Fashion influences from the Cretan people include the **chiton** (KEE ton), consisting of two rectangular pieces of cloth pinned at the shoulder, lacing at the front of the waistline; the puffed and cap sleeve; shift-like undergarments; the bolero jacket; and numerous hat styles.

GREEKS: 700 B.C. TO 53 B.C.

The Greeks were greatly influenced by the Cretans. They adopted the chiton from Cretan dress and the column from Cretan architecture. The form of the column is directly reflected in the chiton (Figure 5–3). The Greeks fashioned these pleated chitons in many colors. Jeweled pins, known as **fibula,** held the chiton on one or both shoulders.

The Doric **peplos** was a woven tubular dress, and the forerunner of today's **peplum.** A peplum is a short section attached to the waistline of a blouse, jacket, or dress. The peplos was woven one foot longer than the wearer's height and twice

Kalasiris

Shenti

Figure 5–2
The shenti was a loincloth worn by Egyptian men. The kalasiris was a linen gown worn by Egyptian women.

the width of the wearer's measurement from elbow to elbow. The folded edges of the Doric peplos were pinned and the garment was belted below the bust and at the waist, creating a blouson effect. A small amount of fabric would extend below the waist, creating a peplum.

The **himation** was the outergarment worn by Greek men and women. It was intricately wrapped about the wearer's shoulders. Social status was implied by the draping used and by the effortless control shown by the wearer in keeping the garment in place.

Dress of Cretan women   Greek chiton

Figure 5–3
As shown on the figure on the left, a Cretan woman's dress was designed to emphasize her small waist. The Cretan people also designed the chiton, a garment consisting of two rectangular pieces of cloth pinned at the shoulder.

ROMANS: 750 B.C. TO 476 A.D.

The Roman people were fashion followers rather than fashion innovators. They adapted fashions of other civilizations to their own lifestyle.

Because of the cold climate, Romans layered their garments. Women wore the **zona,** an undergarment worn below the breasts that was the forerunner of the brassiere. The **tunic,** a shift-like garment, was worn next to the body on top of the zona. Roman men also wore the tunic.

The next layer of clothing was the **toga,** which was adapted from the Etruscans' **tabenna.** The toga was made of a fabric approximately 7 yards × 2½ yards (6.4 meters × 2.3 meters) and cut either in a rectangle, a semicircle, or a folded oval. It was then wrapped around the body, always exposing the right arm and usually covering the left (Figure 5–4). The draping of the toga was so specialized that a slave was frequently needed to assist. Colors were used in the toga to distinguish careers—blue signified a philosopher, white a soothsayer, black a theologian, green a doctor, purple and gold for those of noble birth, and somber colors for the lower classes.[1]

The toga was eventually abandoned by Roman women in favor of the **stola,** which was a long, belted robe similar to the Greek chiton. The stola featured stitched shoulder seams instead of fibula.

The **palla** was the outer garment of Roman women. The men's version was known as the **pallium.** Both fashions were copies of the Greek himation.

Figure 5–4
From 750 B.C. to 476 A.D., Roman men wore draped cloths known as togas.

Romans enjoyed accessories such as gloves, watches (actually miniature sundials), fans, mirrors, and umbrellas. Pearls and emeralds were the preferred jewels.

BYZANTINES: 300 A.D. TO 1453 A.D.

The Byzantine Empire was based in Constantinople on the trade routes linking the East and the West. This is apparent in the Roman and Far Eastern influence in the Byzantine costumes.

The popularity of Christianity at this time is indicated by the fact that the costumes of the royal court concealed the body. Nudity had been quite common before the introduction of Christianity.

The importance of trade with the Orient is reflected in the large amount of silk used in the garments. Silk was imported from China until 550 A.D. when two monks hid the silkworm moth larvae in their hollow pilgrim's staff and smuggled it to Byzantium.[2]

The costume of the Byzantine culture was the **dalmatica,** a long robe with long, loose sleeves. It was usually worn unbelted, or belted high on the body. The dalmatica fitted closely to the upper body and fell to a full skirt. It was later adapted as the dress of the clergy.

FOURTH TO SEVENTH CENTURY A.D.

These were restless times and many people had a nomadic lifestyle which gave them little time to be concerned about their clothing.

The men's costume of this time consisted of two main articles. The **singlet,** a knee-length tunic with a decorative hem worn over pants. A long robe known as a **sagum** was worn over the singlet. The sagum featured embroidered or gold-trimmed edges.

Women wore the **gunna,** a long robe that reached to the floor (Figure 5–5). The gunna featured long, loose sleeves (in Northern Europe) or narrow sleeves (in Byzantium), broad decorative borders at the

Figure 5–5
From the fourth to seventh centuries A.D., women wore long robes known as gunnas.

Gunna

The **Dalmatic tunic** was a common men's garment of the time. Young men wore it thigh-length, older men wore it to the ground. The Dalmatic featured a rounded neck (slit in front), long sleeves, side slits on the skirt, very deep armholes, and elaborate embroidery. It was often seen belted low on the hips.

A thigh-length gunna featuring a full skirt and snug sleeves was also worn by the men. It was belted at the waist, with the top bloused over the belt.

The two most common garments worn by women were the stola and the gunna. The stola was a long, full-skirted dress which was sleeveless and pinned at the shoulder (similar to the chiton). The gunna was a close-fitting, floor-length dress with a low, square neckline. The sleeves were wide, but became tighter as time went on. The gunna was belted.

Hose were quite common accessories on men and women of these centuries. Other accessories included veils, gloves, **chinstraps** (pieces of cloth that fitted under the chin and were pinned at the top of the head), and **headrails** (pieces of fabric worn around the forehead and fastened in back).

TWELFTH TO FIFTEENTH CENTURY A.D.

Two great movements during these centuries had dramatic effects on costuming. The first was the Crusades, which allowed those involved to be exposed to costumes of many lands. The Crusaders' exposure to costumes of eastern cultures resulted in the addition of lavish detailing to western costumes.

The second movement was the beginning of Gothic architecture. The **hennin,** a hat worn by women of the fifteenth century, took on various shapes. One of the shapes was cone-like, a reflection of the spires on the Gothic cathedrals (Figure 5–6).

These were the times of extremity, and the hennin was an example. In order to compete for status, women would lengthen their hennins until it was necessary to have a servant hold the hennin from behind with a pitchfork-like apparatus. Finally, a law was passed that stated the length of a woman's

hem, and often a hood attached to the neckline. If hoods were not attached to the gunna, women would often substitute a veil.

EIGHTH TO TWELFTH CENTURY A.D.

During this portion of the Middle Ages, the feudal system was spreading throughout Europe. The people lived hard lives in towns surrounding castles. Embroidery and weaving flourished among the upper classes as forms of relaxation for the women.

This was the age of knighthood and chivalry. The knights' costume consisted of a woolen tunic which ended slightly below the knee. Over the tunic they wore a shorter tunic made of metal rings for protection. This was known as a **coat of mail.**

Figure 5–6
Worn by women in the twelfth and thirteenth centuries, the bliaud was a two-piece dress with fitted bodice and full sleeves. The hennin, worn in the fifteenth century, was often a cone-like hat resembling spires of a cathedral.

hennin would be determined by the husband's profession.

Extremities also appeared in the footwear of the times. Women donned **chopines** (sho PEENZ), shoes with thickened soles that enabled them to keep their clothing above the dirty streets. Women competed with each other by requesting their chopine soles be built higher and higher, until the shoes were so high that the women could not walk without the help of servants.

The **bliaud,** a two-piece dress featuring a closely fitted bodice, very full skirt, long, full sleeves, and a lowered waistline, was the common costume of women in the twelfth and thirteenth centuries (Figure 5–6). Fine embroidery and smocking were common on the bliaud. Men of the twelfth and thirteenth centuries wore tunics with a **cyclas** (SIK las) on top. The cyclas was a tunic-like garment featuring side seams and deep armholes. **Dagging,** or scalloping, was common as a decorative edging on costumes of both men and women.

The fourteenth century saw heraldry at its peak. Coats of arms featuring family histories were proudly displayed on men as well as on the livery of their horses. Knights were now donning suits of plate armor.

The most common costume of women at this time was the **cotehardie** (koht AH dee), a one-piece dress with a well-fitted bodice, flared skirt, and long, tight sleeves. A **surcoat,** or sideless gown, was worn over the cotehardie. The surcoat was a direct copy of the men's cyclas. The side seams of the surcoat were sewn from the hip to the hem. The church deemed the armholes as the "windows of Hell," thus shortening the life of this fashion.

The fifteenth century brought great interest to costuming. The queens of various lands communicated about their costumes through **court dolls.** These dolls were dressed to emulate the queen of a country and sent to another queen so that she could see the costume of the sender.

As stated earlier, the fifteenth century was a time of extremes. As a sign of beauty, women would shave their eyebrows and their hairline so that there was no visible hair up to the hennin. The women would apply leeches to the skin to create a pallid effect.

The **robe** was the basic women's garment (Figure 5–7). It featured a short-waisted bodice which flattened the bust, a deep square neckline, elaborate interchangeable sleeves, and a floor length, multi-gored skirt with a train. Accessories such as mirrors and keys were attached to a belt. A long, full undergarment known as a **chemise** (shuh MEEZ) was worn under the robe. Following the trend set by Queen Isabella of Castille, women slashed their robes and pulled the chemise out through the slashes, creating a puffed effect.

During this time a tunic was discovered that was believed to have once belonged to the Virgin Mary. The maternal look became fashionable and women of all ages wanted to look pregnant. Thus, a **pregnancy pillow,** stuffed with horsehair and various materials, was tied on underneath the garments (Figure 5–7). Women also walked with their backs arched to make their stomachs protrude further.

The men of this century were not without their eccentricities either. They wore a **jerkin,** a short skirted sleeveless garment with deeply rounded armholes and a dagged hem. Corsets were often worn underneath. Hosiery was an important part of a man's wardrode. At first, the hose were two separate pieces of fabric held up by garters attached to other garments. Eventually, a triangular piece of fabric was attached at the groin to joined the two hose together. This triangular piece was known as the **codpiece** (Figure 5–7). Men began wearing very decorative and exaggerated codpieces. They would stuff them with fabric, or use them as a purse to carry coins.

SIXTEENTH CENTURY

The High Renaissance of the sixteenth century saw fashion at its most splendid, as well as at its most bizarre. The exploration of the New World brought great wealth to Europe. This was mirrored in the beautiful fabrics, laces, precious stones, and furs of the time. Gold thread was commonly woven into fabric, making it extremely stiff and the garments less fluid. Jewels were often affixed to the garments and lace added as a

King Henry VIII wearing a codpiece

Lady's robe and pregnancy pillow

Figure 5–7
Women of the fifteenth century used pregnancy pillows when the maternal look became fashionable. Men of this time wore a codpiece, a decorative triangular piece of fabric attached at the groin.

finishing touch. No one country was the major fashion leader; the countries took turns establishing new looks.

In an effort to temporarily hide her pregnancy from her impotent husband, the wife of Portugal's King Henry V invented the **farthingale** (FAHR thuhn gayl), a stiff metal cone-shaped article worn under the skirt (Figure 5–8). Although it was invented in 1470, it was most popular during the sixteenth century. A wheel-like version of the farthingale was developed by Princess Marguerite of Valois to camouflage her wide hips (Figure 5–8). This style of farthingale become popular in the French and British courts.

Lack of comfort was the price paid for beauty during this century. To achieve their breastless look, women wore iron cages called **vasquines** (vas KEENZ). The vasquines acted as corsets and were held together by bolts. Below the vasquine, the well-dressed woman wore a long pointed apparatus called a **stomacher,** which flattened her stomach.

Perfumes, scented oils, and pomanders were popular because, with no running water, it was hard to keep clean. It's said that Queen Elizabeth I of England had only three baths in her lifetime.[3]

Simple lace-trimmed collars gave way to the **ruff,** a circular face-framing collar (Figure 5–8). Eventually these starched creations became so large that people had to use special elongated eating utensils in order to get food to their mouths. The ruff also hampered movement of the head, so only the higher classes could wear it, thus giving rise to the term "white-collar worker."

Two great queens of this century influenced fashion. They were Elizabeth I of England and Catherine de Medici of France. Both popularized the bell silhouette by wearing farthingales. Catherine de Medici boasted a waistline of only sixteen inches. Additional padding of her hips and sleeves emphasized her wasp waist. She also inspired the Medici collar, a lace ruff which showed much cleavage and which was edged in pearls and gold for formal occasions.

Elizabeth I loved fine garments. At her death she was said to own over 3,000 dresses, many having been gifts from her subjects. She popularized the cartwheel farthingale in England and tall-crowned bonnets with small brims. Her love of pearls revived their use. The loss of her hair prompted the popularity of wigs. If a long-haired wig was worn, women would tuck the hair up into a cap so it wouldn't interfere with the ruff. Accessories, such as masks, fans, rings, and handkerchiefs were important.

During the sixteenth century, menswear began to take on the appearance of the garments that men wear today. The **pourpoint** (POOR point), a forerunner of today's shirt, was the major men's garment. It featured a high standing collar, set-in sleeves, center front closure, and a short, full peplum.[4] A doublet was often worn over the pourpoint. Slashing was common on all men's garments, including the codpiece and hose. A **bases,** or skirt-like article, was tied around the waist and usually extended to the knee.

Men's hosiery began to change in the middle of the century when the upper and lower hose became separate and more clearly defined. The lower hose were now knitted and close fitting, while the upper hose were padded and slashed. **Pumpkin breeches** were well-padded upper hose and were so named because they resembled pumpkins. **Venetians,** another style of upper hose, were introduced in Venice. They were loosely fitted knee-length breeches resembling the knickers of today.

SEVENTEENTH CENTURY

The plague of 1665 and the fire of 1666 kept England's mind off fashion for a time, and the French began to gain prestige. France became the world's fashion leader under the rule of the "Sun King," Louis XIV. France became the center of textile production and fashion innovation. Those attending parties at Louis' grand palace at Versailles determined fashion trends by what they wore.

At the beginning of the seventeenth century, menswear was little changed from the previous century. Pumpkin breeches and venetians were still worn. The ruff was

Spanish farthingale

English farthingale

Ruff

Figure 5–8
*The farthingale was a stiff metal cone-shaped article worn under skirts by women during the sixteenth century.
The ruff, a large stiff collar, was also popular.*

replaced by a flat, lace-edged collar known as a **whisk.** Lace became an important addition to men's garments. In general, men's wear developed an air of femininity, complemented by the long and wavy hairstyles for men.

As the century progressed, trousers were less stuffed and were fitted closer to the leg, with lace at the knee. Shirts, which were cut fuller, became more visible. These shirts featured full long sleeves and were often embroidered or trimmed with little bows made of ribbon. Popular accessories for men included swords, spurs, capes, and garters.

The middle of the century saw the development of **rhinegraves,** also known as **petticoat breeches,** which were designed by Louis XIV's tailors. These gathered breeches were worn over well-padded upper hose, with lace trim at their hem. They were so full that they often resembled skirts, not pants. The breeches were feminine and elaborate, some sporting hundreds of yards of ribbon on a single pair. A **cravat,** or lace-edged rectangular piece of linen, encircled the neck and was tied in a bow or knot.

Louis XIV lost his hair because of a severe illness and wigs became popular for men. Louis XIV's wigs were high in an effort to make him look taller. Powdering wigs with talc became popular near the end of the century.

The beginning of the seventeenth century also saw little change in women's costume, but by 1620 women became disenchanted with hoops and rolls. For the first time in a hundred years, fabric fell naturally from the waist to the hem.[5] Women often displayed color in their garments by slashing the front of their outer skirt and attaching it at the hips, revealing the underskirt. This fashion was named for its originator, Madame Fontange (FON tahnzh), a mistress to Louis XIV, and was called the **Fontange silhouette.**

The ruff remained popular for women and the necklines became even lower. Hairstyles became massive, making it necessary to wear hats cocked to the side of the head. A small cap which fitted over the head was developed for mourning. Called a **widow's peak,** it featured a deep point on the forehead and a long veil on the back of the cap. The term "widow's peak" is still used today to denote a natural hairline that comes to a point on the forehead.

Beauty marks were applied to areas of the face to signify various personality traits. A women could convey passion, flirtation, or boldness simply by where she placed her beauty mark.[6]

Other popular accessories of the time included muffs of fur or fabric, fur scarves, fans, masks, gloves, pomanders, mirrors, and eye patches.

EIGHTEENTH CENTURY

The grand designs of the seventeenth century were abandoned in the eighteenth for lighter and more delicate colors and patterns. Interest in men's fashions slowed as Louis XIV aged. On his death in 1715, new life was breathed into fashion. The cravat was replaced by the **stock,** a neckband which tied in front and had a frilly extension under the collar known as a **jabot** (zha BOH).

A suit coat known as a **redingote** (RED ing goht), or **justaucorps** (ZHEUS toh kaw) was very popular (Figure 5–9). The forerunner of today's suit coat, it featured a fitted waist and flared skirt. As the century progressed, the coat became thigh-length, with a higher neckline and less fabric and lace at the neckline, cuffs, and skirt. Fur or braid were common decorative touches. Shirts featuring narrow collars that turned over the stock were commonly worn under the redingote.

Wigs became less popular as the century progressed. Eventually men brushed their hair back from the head and tied it at the nape or curled a few locks above the ears.

The French Revolution brought on outlandish fashions, reflecting the unrest of the times. The redingote became so tight that the buttons could no longer be fastened. Long tails were added to the back, a high turnover collar and wide lapels were popular, and buttons were applied in a double-breasted manner. Trousers were completely visible and ankle length.

The young people of the French Revolution protested the elegant lifestyle of

Spencer jacket

Justaucorps

Figure 5–9
The eighteenth-century justaucorps was a forerunner of today's suitcoat. The Spencer jacket was a short jacket without tails.

Louis XVI's court. The young men were known as *Incroyables* (an krwah YAHBL), which is French for "incredible," and the young women as *Merveilleuses* (mehr vay YURZ), French for "marvellous." The Incroyables wore exaggerated garments in mockery of the French Court of Louis XVI. Their garments were wrinkled to give them a slept-in look, cravats were carelessly tied, and lapels were ridiculously large. Their trousers were long, loose creations known as **culottes** (French for "pants").

A short, tailless jacket was popularized by Lord Spencer of England. Appropriately, it was named the **Spencer jacket** (Figure 5–9). One story states that it was developed when Lord Spencer was thrown from his horse, ripping off the tails. Another story attributes the design to the fact that Lord Spencer once stood too close to a fire and burned off his coattails.

At the beginning of the eighteenth century, women of the French Court dominated fashion. Louis XV's mistress,

Madame de Pompadour, was graceful, cultured, and a lover of the arts. She was faithful to the French way of dress, while adding her own influence. She began the fashion of wearing bows on the stomacher and at the elbow and of having frilled neckbands. She edged her neckline with a lace known as *tatez-y* (tah tay ZEE), which is French for "touch here." She combed her hair straight back from the brow, with a lift. Thus, the **pompadour** hairstyle began.

As the century continued, the bell silhouette became more horizontal; skirts were hooped again and necklines became wider. The hoops were no longer circular, but rather flattened in the front and back. The **pannier** (PAHN yair) was an undergarment which supported the skirts on the sides. It was tied to a woman's waist, creating the desired wide effect without the need for hoops. Panniers were made of cane or whalebone and through various tying methods could extend as far as the wearer pleased. Panniers became so wide that hinges were often added so that the wearer could lift them to enter a doorway or carriage.

The eighteenth century was a time of femininity. Women's hairstyles were soft, with loose curls at the back of the head and longer curls falling over the shoulders. Live flowers were used as accessories. Garlands were placed at the neckline and hem, as well as in the hair. Small pockets were sewn into the garment's lining to hold water vials to keep the flowers from wilting. It was recorded that Marie Antoinette (wife of Louis XVI) wore a gown that had the entire skirt covered with fresh flowers.

Fabrics worn by the wealthy were elaborate. Gowns were of damask, taffeta, gold or silk brocade, or silver cloth. French painter Jean Antoine Watteau (Wah TOH) influenced the style for gowns of the French Court through his paintings. He depicted women in gowns with full flowing trains falling from the back shoulder line, creating back interest in the garment's silhouette. This innovation was known as the **Watteau neckline.**

Under the influence of Marie Antoinette, ladies' hair again became high and powdered. Often a padded structure supported the hair from inside. Powder was applied with shakers and bellows. A flour paste was added to give whiteness to the powder. During the French Revolution, peasants complained that the flour used on hairstyles lessened their food supply. The extravagant hairstyles took many shapes including carriages, ships, garden scenes, people, or current events. Hygiene suffered for the sake of beauty. Head lice were common because the hair creations would stay intact from three to four weeks. If the lice became too active, servants would slit an opening in the hair, remove as many lice as possible, and mend the slit.

The end of the century saw many changes in women's costumes. Panniers became smaller then finally disappeared, although the French Court retained hoops. Panniers were replaced by the **bustle,** a padded or wired device that was worn over the wearer's posterior.

Women adopted the men's redingote as an overcoat or dress. The women's redingote was tailored and well-fitted, featuring deep collars and wide lapels. The Spencer coat was also adapted for women.

The Merveilleuses wore a Grecian-style garment of muslin, featuring a high waistline. The garment was known as the **chemise gown.** The waistline was known as the **empire,** named after the French Empire of Napoleon's reign.

The eighteenth century saw an interest in Greek sculpture. Women's garments followed classic Greek lines as shown in the "Victory of Samothrace" sculpture (Figure 5–10). The popularity of these garments was attributed to the fact that they were in such contrast to the dress of the French Court. It was unthinkable to the peasants to dress as the much-hated royalty did. The muslin creations resembled chitons and were often worn without undergarments to shock others. To further duplicate the look of "Victory of Samothrace," women would dampen their garments so they would cling to the body. Laws were finally passed restricting this practice because of the resulting deaths from pneumonia. The clean lines of the Greek-inspired garments left no room for pockets, so women carried purses known as **indispensables.**

Hairstyles consisted of short ringlet curls, to further emulate early-day Greeks. A

"Victory of Samothrace sculpture"

Dress fashioned after Greek sculpture

Figure 5–10
Women's garments of the eighteenth century followed the classic lines of Greek sculpture.

touch of sardonic humor was added by the Merveilleuses in the red ribbon they wore around their necks to represent the cut of the guillotine.[7]

NINETEENTH CENTURY

The nineteenth century began with the continuation of the French Revolution. Eventually, the revolution caused a reorganization of society and the rise of the middle class. This had a direct effect on

fashion in that all classes began to dress similarly.

France lost its position as head of textile production during the revolution, and England took over. On Napoleon's coronation as Emperor, however, France regained its lead. Unlike Louis XIV, Napoleon did not strive to make France the leading textile producer merely because he loved fashion. He saw the economic benefit to France.

Significant changes took place in the fashion world during the nineteenth century. In 1840, *Godey's Lady's Book*—the first fashion magazine—was published, simplifying the task of communicating fashion. In 1846, the sewing machine was invented, forever changing the fashion industry.

At the end of the French monarchy, men's fashions lost their color and magnificence, except for the garments worn in Napoleon's court.

In 1800, the first ready-to-wear shops appeared in the United States. By the end of the century most custom-tailoring businesses had gone out of business.

The English displayed their fine cutting and tailoring techniques, beautiful fabrics, and sense of grooming during the nineteenth century. It was the age of the **dandies,** or well-dressed men, and their leader was George "Beau" Brummel (Figure 5–11). Although Brummel did not create fashion trends, he adapted them to his liking. He led men's fashion from 1796 to 1816, introducing shoe polish, clean linen daily, and the starching of cravats.

Men no longer wore knee breeches and pants reached the ankle. Before 1815, pants were so tight they were made of knit fabric to allow movement. In time, pants loosened up at the hips and added a **fly,** or front closure.

Shirts of the time were no longer edged with lace. Instead, they were ruffled down the front and featured a high collar. A folded cravat was tied at the neck. A **waistcoat,** a forerunner to the vest, was worn over the shirt. It featured a standing collar and a low single-breasted closing. Over the waistcoat, men wore double-breasted coats with tails. They wore their hair shorter and curled, and sported sideburns that often extended to the chin. Accessories were important to men in the first half of the century. Some of the most common were gloves, watch fobs, and top hats.

As the century continued, the dandy flourished and men again took on a feminine look. This look included a protruding chest, pinched waist (achieved with corsets), and rounded hips. Trousers followed the feminine trend with tight waistbands and delicate pleating at the waistline to make the hips look larger.

The tailcoat was worn in the evening or for formal wear. In daytime, it was replaced by the **frock coat,** which had an even hem length at the knees and leg-of-mutton sleeves that ended in a tight wrist. The waistcoat was still quite popular and highly decorated. The neckline became lowered and a shawl collar was added. The cravat was now tied in a flat bow around removable collars. The removable collar was invented by a blacksmith's wife who was tired of providing her husband with a clean shirt daily.

An important fashion trend began midcentury with the matching of a man's coat, waistcoat, and trousers. These outfits were known as **ditto suits.** Previously, the trousers, waistcoat, and coat had used contrasting colors. It was also common to see checks and plaids in men's daytime wear at this time.

By 1870, print shirts had been introduced into men's wardrobes, with polka dots and stripes being quite popular. The collar of the shirt now turned over at the corner for comfort. This collar was known as the **wing collar,** or **gates ajar.**

Popular accessories of the time included fedoras, top hats, bowlers, straw boaters, a cloth and rubber shoe (forerunner to the tennis shoe), neckties with collegiate stripes, patent leather spats, monocles, gloves, and walking sticks.

Sports became important in men's leisure time. Specific garments were created for such sports as tennis, swimming, hunting, and mountain climbing.

Edward VII of England was trying on pants in a tailor's shop. When he tried on a pair which had creased legs (from being folded for sometime), he was pleased with the slenderizing effect of the creases. Thus began a fashion detail that continues through today.

The Greek influence still dominated women's garments of the early nineteenth century, although undergarments and some corsets were repopularized. The waistline continued to be raised and controlled by a drawstring. The Empress Josephine, Napoleon's wife, wore elaborate versions of this gown in heavier, printed fabrics.

The simplicity of Greek-inspired costumes gave attention to headdresses. Many forms were worn including encircled vines, berets, turbans, and straw hats in various designs.

Eventually dresses became less revealing

Figure 5–11
The well-dressed man of nineteenth-century England was called a dandy. The well-dressed woman wore a large bell-shaped skirt supported by a crinoline. The Worth creation brought the fullness of women's skirts around to the back.

Worth creation

Bell silhouette with crinoline

Nineteenth century dandy

at the bustline and the skirts achieved a fuller effect. The Greek influence had more or less disappeared by 1820. Luxurious fabrics in bright colors became very popular. Fullness was added to the garment's sleeves (leg-of-mutton) and skirts (were pleated or gathered). For a short time the bust reappeared. To stay in proportion, huge hats became the rage. The hats, known as **picture hats,** were bedecked in bows, ribbons, birds, and lace.

The necklines continued in their horizontal line until the shoulder area was bared. Sleeves and skirts continued to become fuller and waistlines were lowered, emphasizing the bell silhouette (Figure 5–11). The sleeves were supported by boning or cushions. Skirts were supported by **crinolines,** which were bell-shaped stiff undergarments of wool and horsehair or by petticoats. The tiny waists the women flaunted were achieved by painful lacing.

Dresses eventually became as fussy and cluttered as the ladies' Victorian homes. The dresses presented a wide, low look that complemented the low, heavy Victorian furniture of the times.

Romance flourished mid-century and women were prudish and fainted easily. The fainting may have been caused by hunger. It was considered distasteful for women to eat in public, so many went without food. The massive weight of the garments along with the tight lacing at the waist may also have caused women to faint.

By 1844, sleeves became straight and narrower, and necklines moved up the shoulder line to form a V-shape. Hats became small and modest.

The 1850s saw the beginning of many fashion changes. Empress Eugénie, Napoleon III's wife, set many fashion trends aided by her designer, Charles Worth (see Chapter 6). Eugénie popularized the bolero jacket, the felt hat, and Scottish tartans. She also made crinolines popular.[8] Eventually, crinolines were replaced by a Worth creation—a multi-gored skirt that swept the excess fullness to the back, allowing freer movement (Figure 5–11).

Mrs. Amelia Bloomer, editor of a feminist newspaper, started the trend of **bloomers,** which were loose trousers gathered at the ankle. They were usually worn with skirts that were mid-calf length, allowing the bloomers to show below the hem. This was a popular style for bicycling, but was opposed by antifeminists who considered the style masculine.

In 1869, the bustle reappeared, again distorting the female shape. The overskirt was slashed, pulled up and attached at the bustle, to expose the underskirt.

The bustle eventually became smaller during the last decade of the 1800s. The female figure began to resemble an hourglass through widening of the sleeves and tighter corsets at the waistline. To maintain a small waistline, some women went to the extreme of having lower ribs surgically removed. Women also developed a new stance, known as the **monobosom** look, in which they leaned forward.

Artist Charles Dana Gibson immortalized the young fashion-conscious woman of this decade in his paintings. She was thus known as the **Gibson Girl** (Figure 5–12).

TWENTIETH CENTURY

During the nineteenth century, fashions evolved and changed slowly. The twentieth century, in contrast, brought constant change. At no other time had fashion designers been so conspicuous. Important influences on fashion included the cinema, television, World War II, the Space Program, youth, and the women's movement.

At the beginning of the century, women's garments became more tailored. The bustline continued to protrude and the waistline was still controlled by the corset. These facts, as well as the forward stance exhibited, prompted the style to be known as the **S shape** because the body resembled the letter "S."

The invention of the automobile called for an appropriate costume, and the **dustcoat** was born. Roads were dry and dirty, so women wore dustcoats to protect their garments (Figure 5–13). To further fight the dust, women wore boots, goggles, and large hats with veils to cover the face.

As 1910 approached, the hourglass figure continued but without the "S" stance or the protruding bust. French designer Paul Poiret introduced the **hobble skirt,** so

The Depression struck in 1929 and hemlines became longer. The unsure times also spawned the uneven "handkerchief" hemline, a reflection of the shaky economy. Home sewing was at an all-time high, since women couldn't afford to buy garments.

The 1930s saw the waistline rise and women dieted to achieve a long, thin look. Wide slacks, known as **trousers,** and shorts above the knee were worn for sporting events. Backless garments appeared in evening wear, as well as bathing suits. Evening gowns were long, form-fitting, and often cut on the bias (Figure 5–15), a style popularized by actress Jean Harlow. "Streamline" was the term for this decade, as seen in the women's thin bodies, tight garments, and art deco jewelry.

The onset of World War II brought many changes to women's costumes. The

The Gibson girl

Figure 5–12
The fashion-conscious woman of the nineteenth century became known as the Gibson girl after being immortalized by painter Charles Dana Gibson.

named because it was so narrow that the wearer couldn't walk and had to hobble (Figure 5–14).

After World War I women became more active and the hobble skirt, considered too confining, disappeared. The women's movement had women competing with men. There were important items for this new competition, including middy blouses with sailor collars, and sweaters. Women also participated in sports, using bloomers as a gym costume.[9]

With the 1920s came the Age of Jazz, the Charleston, and the flapper, with her dropped waist, tubular dress, long pearl necklace, and bobbed hair. Undergarments included camisoles, panties, teddies, and brassieres that flattened the bust for an even more masculine, tubular effect. Flappers applied cosmetics and eye make-up freely for a dramatic effect.

Dustcoat

Figure 5–13
At the beginning of the twentieth century, women wore dustcoats to protect their clothing when driving in cars.

Hobble skirt

Figure 5–14
This narrow skirt got its name because it constricted women's movement, causing them to hobble.

occupation of France forced the great fashion houses of Chanel, Vionnet, and Dior to close temporarily. Women reflected a "uniform" look with broad padded shoulders, shorter full skirts, and nipped-in waistlines (Figure 5–16). Because of the hard times inflicted by World War II, any show of wealth or flamboyancy was considered tasteless.

In 1942, the United States government passed Law L-85 which had a tremendous effect on design and production, and furthered the uniformity of fashion. The law set the following standards for garment manufacturing:

- no patch pockets
- a maximum of 2-inch (5-centimeter) hems
- no cuffs on pants
- a maximum of 3½ yards (3 meters) of fabric per garment

- no metal closings (because metal was needed for the war effort)

In 1947, after World War II ended, a dramatic event occurred in the fashion industry. Designer Christian Dior, on reopening his house in Paris, introduced a style he called the **New Look.** It featured natural shoulders, small waistline, and a longer, very full skirt (Figure 5–16). After the uniformity of the early 1940s and the end of Law L-85, women happily accepted the New Look. That was the only time in history that hemlines literally changed overnight.

The 1950s were an era of fun in women's fashions. Many actresses set fashion trends and extremes. Marilyn Monroe and Jayne Mansfield brought attention to the full bustline with the help of the **Merry Widow,** an undergarment that pulled the waist in and pushed the bust up. Actress Audrey

"Streamline" gown

Figure 5–15
Tight form-fitting garments were the popular fashion for women during the 1930s.

Dior's New Look

World War II woman's suit

Figure 5–16
This Christian Dior suit introduced a dramatic new look for women.

Hepburn set the other extreme, making the undernourished look fashionable by pulling her hair back into a ponytail and wearing black leotards and ballet slippers.

Dior also brought about new fashion looks in the 1950s. His designs included the A-line silhouette known as the **trapeze** dress and the H-line dress which was low-waisted.

Ladies' skirts were full at this time. They used a minimum of 4 yards (3.6 meters) of fabric and were supported by crinolines and hoops. Slacks came in various lengths and had various names. Clam diggers and pedal pushers were common for sports and after-school wear. Gloves were popular accessories, with different lengths and styles for different occasions.

Fashions of the youth in the mid- to late-fifties were influenced by such performers as Elvis Presley, James Dean, and Marlon Brando. Their influence was seen in leather jackets, pompadour hairstyles, dungarees, and white T-shirts.

Young women adopted two-piece garments, either a skirt and sweater combination or an excessively large shirt (often a man's white shirt) worn over a pair of cuffed jeans.

Television and movies of the 1950s inspired children's clothing. There were Roy Rogers and Dale Evans fashions, as well as Davy Crockett coonskin caps. Teenagers watched American Bandstand on television to see what their favorite teens were wearing.

In menswear, the 1950s were known as the "Man in the Gray Flannel Suit" era, a term derived from a book by Sloan Wilson. The look for young men was Ivy League—button-down oxford shirts, oxford shoes, and narrow regimental ties. For men out of college, the uniform was a gray sack-cut suit with narrow lapels, striped tie, wing-tip oxford shoes, and a gray fedora hat (Figure 5–17).

The first strong fashion innovator of the 1960s was first lady, Jacqueline Kennedy. The clean-cut simplicity of her style was accepted and copied by women of all economic levels (Figure 5–18). The Jackie look consisted of either a two-piece suit (or a dress with a short jacket), or a Chanel-style suit (often double-breasted) with a rounded neckline. While dresses were often sleeveless, jackets sported three-quarter length sleeves year round. A-line skirts hit at, or just below, the knee. The Jackie follower also wore low-heeled pumps. Her evening dresses featured high empire waistlines. Other Jackie trademarks were the bouffant hairdo, the pillbox hat, and large buttons. The buttons were 2 inches (5 centimeters) in diameter and placed (often singularly but never more than two) at the throat.[10]

For the junior customer of the 1960s, the trend setter was English designer Mary Quant and her **mini skirt** creation of 1962. The eye was now drawn from the bosom of the 1950s to the leg of the 1960s. The mini was short and straight. Garter belts became a thing of the past and pantyhose were developed since women needed hosiery that would complement the mini.

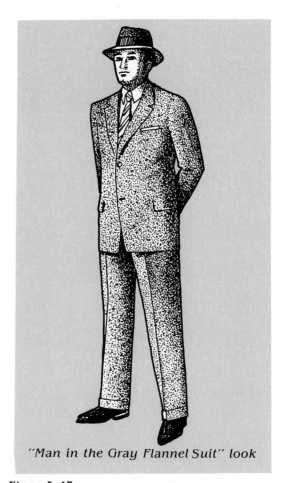

"Man in the Gray Flannel Suit" look

Figure 5–17
The uniform for young men out of college in the 1950s consisted of a gray suit with narrow lapels, striped tie, oxford shoes, and gray fedora hat.

The Jackie look

Figure 5–18
First lady Jacqueline Kennedy started a clean-cut fashion trend which was followed by women of all economic levels.

The Beatles came to the United States in 1964 and the British influence invaded fashion as well as music. The art world was flooded with bright, bold prints and optics including dots and stripes. This modern art influenced the "Mod" fashion look, also known as the "Carnaby Street" look, and was best expressed by British models Jean "the Shrimp" Shrimpton and Lesley "Twiggy" Hornsby. French designer André Courrèges added the finishing touch with his white "go-go" boots. A shocking touch to fashion came at this time with California designer Rudi Gernreich's transparent blouses and topless bathing suits.

French designer Yves Saint Laurent introduced the tailored women's pantsuit in 1966, to the delight of women. The pantsuit brought comfort to women, a luxury not achieved with the miniskirt. At first, pantsuits were not accepted for all occasions

and women in pantsuits were not allowed in some restaurants. This, of course, changed.

In 1969 hemlines were uncertain. Was it the mini, the midi, or the maxi? Many women stuck to pantsuits until the decision was made: the shorter mini remained in favor, and the midi and maxi soon disappeared from retail stores.

The 1960s also saw the **Hippie look** for both men and women. It consisted of jeans—decorated with patches, paint, silver studs, or embroidery—and a chambray workshirt, also well decorated. Bras were temporarily discarded. Finishing off the look was the accessory of the day—love beads. See Figure (5–19). Rock stars, including Janis Joplin, Jimi Hendrix, and Jefferson Airplane, were the fashion leaders of the 1960s.

Formal menswear of the 1960s was strongly influenced by Italian designers, but the youth rebellion had a strong effect on casual menswear. The trend was the sloppy, anti-establishment look. The men wore their hair longer, and suits and ties disappeared. Bright colors also found their way into men's wardrobes.

In the 1970s, the dandy appeared in men's fashions. Men wore bright colors in shiny polyesters and cottons. In the early 70s, large butterfly bow ties were popular, as well as wide collars and wide neckties.

Polyester went to the extreme in the **leisure suit,** a two-piece suit for men. It consisted of slacks and a jacket featuring a large collar and topstitching. A bright floral shirt was typically worn beneath the jacket, without a necktie, with the shirtcollar rolled over the jacket collar. The look was casual. Some people considered the leisure suit to be men's fashion at its worst.

At this time, stars and stripes resembling the American flag were printed on clothing for both sexes. In addition, the T-shirt came to life for both men and women. White was abandoned in favor of bright colors and slogans were printed on the front.

Women of the early '70s wore **hot pants,** a collaboration of the mini skirt and pantsuit. Jeans were still popular, but now in the low **hiphugger** style, with the waistband on the hipbone. Clunky platform shoes were the accessory of the day. The hot pants were the last breath of the

The hippie look

Figure 5—19
An important style for young men and women of the 1960s consisted of jeans decorated with embroidery, a patched or embroidered workshirt, and lovebeads.

outlandish look from the 1960s.

The romantic Edwardian look became fashionable in a new long length. Millions of Gunne Sax dresses, by California designer Jessica McClintock, were sold to women of all ages—not only for prom dresses but also for wedding dresses and daytime wear.

Jeans were still popular, but now they sported bleach spots, embroidery, and tie-dye. Often old jeans were cut up and

fashioned into a new patchwork pair. By 1973, classic feminine styling was back for women. American designer Diane Von Furstenberg popularized the versatile jersey **wrap dress.**

John T. Molloy set the standards of correct office attire for both sexes in his *Dress For Success* books. The professional look included classic suits for men and women, natural fibers, and neutral colors. More women joined the work force at this time, making classic styling popular. The economic recession encouraged classic styles because women were less likely to spend their money on fashion fads. They needed classics that would endure.

The popularity of the movie *Saturday Night Fever* spawned the **disco look** for both sexes. *Annie Hall* popularized the baggy, layered look for women. *Star Wars* encouraged the wearing of capes, flat boots, and lurex threads in fabrics. *Grease* popularized the look of the 1950s, including argyle sweaters and saddle shoes.

Some trends have already made definite impacts in the 1980s. American designers Calvin Klein and Gloria Vanderbilt became household names through the designer jean craze of the '80s.

The film *Urban Cowboy* popularized the western and prairie looks. *Chariots of Fire* inspired a romantic look of the 1920s, including a dropped waistline on women's garments. *Amadeus* brought brocades and ruffled jabots to fashion, while *Flashdance* inspired the ripped sweatshirt look.

The shoulders are of definite interest in the 1980s, with even more padding than in the '40s. Resurrected by American designer Norma Kamali, shoulder pads are still going strong. Kamali also made cotton fleece "sweat" fabric fashionable.

Proper dress for women executives was as important during the first half of the 1980s as during the '70s, but more colorful and exciting than the "Molloy Clones" of the '70s. American designer, Liz Claiborne, made her mark in the 1980s because she met the needs of the working woman.

The fashion market of the '80s was also influenced by the **punk look,** which originated in England (Figure 5—20), the neutral multi-layered look of Japan, and the master tailoring of Italy (Figure 5—21). First lady Nancy Reagan also influenced the fashion market with her clean lines and favorite color, red. England's Princess Diana set trends with her haircut, high ruffled collars, flat heeled shoes, hats, gloves, and delicate clean lines.

A strong interest in physical fitness continues into the 1980s. Actress Jane Fonda developed an exercise video, along with a line of exercise fashions. Jogging

The punk look

Figure 5—20
The punk look influenced fashion in the '80s.

suits and running shoes are part of the fitness craze. And not only are the sports participants appropriately attired, but so are the spectators.

Rock videos have influenced the fashions of the younger generation. Young viewers take note of the fashion trends of Cyndi Lauper (old clothes, rags, multiple accessories), Madonna (lace), Prince (his hairstyle, his purple clothing, and open shirt), Boy George (his hat and multi-layered fashions), and Michael Jackson (the

Japanese layering

Italian tailoring

Figure 5—21
Two influential styles of the 1980s.

quilted leather coat, black shoes with white or silver socks, and the silver glove).

The study of history's reflection on the world of fashion isn't new. It is important to understand the cyclical movement of fashion and how current events affect styles. Wise fashion designers and retail fashion buyers are up-to-date on current world and local events so they can predict how the public will respond to fashions.

Projects

1. Study contemporary clothing. Research the changes in men's and women's clothing from 1947 to now. Write and illustrate a report, using original drawings and clippings.
2. Construct a Costume History Time Line and fill in the important dates, events, and fashions from the time of ancient Egyptian costume to now.
3. Choose a period in history. Research it thoroughly and write a report on the mode of dress for that period. Include footnotes, a bibliography, and illustrations.
4. Look through fashion magazines of the twentieth century. Pick five fashions of the twentieth century. Discuss how fashions of previous centuries have influenced the current designs.

6
Fashion Designers

It takes more than drawing ability to become a successful fashion designer. One must understand design principles, fabrics, and construction techniques, as well as be able to predict what clients desire.

Identifying fashion trends is important in creating successful designs. Designers must know their **target market**—those who are likely to buy their designs. Otherwise, their garments are not likely to sell.

Different designers often show similar styles within a season because their inspirations come from common sources, such as current events. Other sources for inspiration are forecasting services such as I.M. International, current films, previous design collections, other designers, trade publications such as *Women's Wear Daily*, consumer publications such as *Vogue* magazine, historic costume collections and books, and entertainers.

For decades, designers mainly worked for design corporations. This changed in the 1970s with more and more designers owning their own businesses. This gave them more interest in their designs, as well as greater profits. Another relatively new aspect of the design business is **licensing**—when a designer sells the use of his or her name to a manufacturer.

This chapter outlines those designers considered the fashion greats of all time. They are presented in alphabetical order for easy reference. Their birth names, birthdate, work history, and contributions are noted.

GILBERT ADRIAN

Adrian Adolph Greenburg
1903 to 1960
American designer

American designer Adrian studied at Parson's School of Design in Manhattan and later in Paris. He began his fashion career as a Broadway designer for Irving Berlin and Flo Ziegfeld. Relocating to Hollywood in 1923, he eventually became MGM's head fashion designer. He left MGM in 1942 to begin his own design company.

While at MGM, Adrian designed for Rosalind Russell, Greta Garbo, Judy Garland, Norma Shearer, Joan Crawford, and his wife Janet Gaynor.

He was known for detailed designs including insets, padded shoulders, dolman sleeves, and diagonal closures.

ADOLFO

Adolfo Sardina
1929 to
American designer

Cuban-born Adolfo began his career as an apprentice to Balenciaga in France. In 1948, he relocated to New York City and designed millinery. He opened his own firm in the early 1960s and expanded to ladies' fashions.

His popular millinery styles included large berets made of fur and the Panama hat of 1966. In clothing, he offers romantic evening wear as well as crisply tailored suits worn often by first lady Nancy Reagan.

GIORGIO ARMANI

1936 to
Italian designer

Known as the master tailor of Italy, Armani attended medical school for three years and was a medical assistant in the Italian army. After his army duties were over, he took a job first as a window decorator, and then as an assistant buyer with La Rinascente, a department store in Milan. On leaving retail, he became a design assistant for Nino Cerruti.

Armani opened his own design company in 1970. He is known for finely tailored menswear, women's jackets patterned after men's, the wrinkled look, unconstructed jackets, and the reintroduction of linen to men's and women's fashions.

CRISTOBAL BALENCIAGA

1895 to 1972
French designer

Considered by many as one of the greatest designers of all time, Balenciaga was born and raised in Spain. As a young boy he was befriended by Marquesa de Casa Torres, who allowed him to copy a designer suit she owned. Recognizing his talent, she later paid Balenciaga's way to Paris so he could see couture first-hand. She also provided him with financial backing to open his own design business in Spain. This was eventually relocated in Paris where such fashion notables as Courrèges, Ungaro, and Givenchy trained under Balenciaga, "The Master."

Among Balenciaga's design innovations are narrow, rolled collars higher in front than in back, large bow details, a jutting well-defined peplum, the sack dress, strapless evening gowns in black, patterned hosiery woven in heavier fibers for warmth, the repopularization of the chemise, the semi-fitted jacket, evening gowns featuring a slight train in back, cocoon coats, and loose jackets worn over box-pleated skirts.

GEOFFREY BEENE

1927 to
American designer

Beene first studied medicine at Tulane University, but started drawing fashions onto the anatomical sketches. A psychiatrist helped him realize that medicine was not his calling. He then moved to Paris to study art and became intrigued with fabrics. After working for many American designers, he opened his own business in 1962. Now he licenses products such as sheets, hosiery, and fashionable eyewear.

Beene is known for eccentricity at his showings, such as sweatshirt evening gowns and sequined football jerseys. He uses elegant natural fibers in quiet colors.

ROSE BERTIN

Marie Jeanne Laurent Bertin
1747 to 1813
French designer

The first famous designer, Bertin gained fame as Marie Antoinette's official dressmaker. She designed both headdresses and gowns before the French Revolution. Her opulent designs were not limited to Marie Antoinette, but also went to other foreign courts.

MR. BLACKWELL

Richard Blackwell
Birthdate not available
American designer

Mr. Blackwell, known for his sharp tongue and ready-to-wear designs, added fun to the fashion industry with his annual "Ten Worst Dressed List," which began in 1960. His "List," from which no notable is safe, has included Cher, Brooke Shields, Bo Derek, Caroline Kennedy, and Raquel Welch.

Blackwell began his show business career as one of the original "Dead End Kids" and appeared on Broadway with Mae West. He eventually moved to California while under contract with Howard Hughes. He left the stage to manage talent and received notice for the designs he created for the personalities he managed. In 1955 he and Robert Spencer formed Mr. Blackwell designs, mainly a dress and suit line.

BILL BLASS

1922 to
American designer

Known as the "Mayor of Seventh Avenue," Blass began by studying art in New York and working as the sketch artist for a sportswear company. After a tour of duty during World War II, he was offered a design position with Anna Miller. There he received recognition when an editor at *Vogue* featured his designs in an article.

In 1959, Blass went to work for designer Maurice Rentner, became vice-president in 1961, and owned the company ten years later. Through his company he licenses products such as bedding, fragrance, and Lincoln Continental automobiles.

Blass' collections have featured such innovations as long, lean evening gowns, sable-trimmed pink cashmere coats, and clean-cut architectural shapes.

ALBERT CAPRARO

1943 to
American designer

Famous for his feminine, yet classic detailing, Capraro associated with such fashion greats as Lilly Daché and Oscar de la Renta before opening his own design company in 1974.

Capraro's garments have been worn by such notables as first lady Betty Ford and Christina Ferrare DeLorean. He made headlines by designing Mrs. DeLorean's courtroom wardrobe, which she wore during her husband's much-publicized trial.

PIERRE CARDIN

Pierre Cardini
1922 to
French designer

Italian-born Cardin began his career working for a clothier in Vichy, Italy. On his arrival in Paris, he worked for Paquin, and then joined Dior in 1946. In 1950, he opened his own design firm.

The first designer to make a licensing agreement, Cardin is called the "King of Licensing." In the mid-1980s he held over 500 licenses, ranging from airplanes to children's clothing.

Considered a great tailor in his couture line, Cardin is known for popularizing tights. His other contributions include tailored jerseys worn with bulky sweaters, the space-age look, metal body jewelry, and jumpsuits with batwing sleeves.

GABRIELLE "COCO" CHANEL

1883 to 1971
French designer

At age 20, Chanel worked as a nightclub singer and dancer and met an Englishman who gave her money to begin a hat shop in Paris. Designing hats gave way to designing garments after World War I. The bombing of Paris during World War II forced Chanel to close her house and retire. She came out of retirement in 1953. The House of Chanel continues today under the direction of Karl Lagerfeld.

Chanel made many contributions to the fashion industry including the classic "little black dress," man-sized sweaters worn by women, sailor's pea coats worn over a straight pleated skirt, and the jersey as an outer garment. She also popularized slacks for women, neutral colors, the little boy look, bell-bottom slacks, and the Chanel pump (beige and black sling back).

LIZ CLAIBORNE

1930 to
American designer

Belgium-born Claiborne grew up in New Orleans and studied art and painting in Paris and Brussels. Her design career was launched when she entered and won a design contest by *Harper's Bazaar* magazine. Later, Claiborne moved to New York where she designed for Jonathan Logan for 16 years.

In 1976, Claiborne began her own company with her husband Arthur Ortenberg, a textile expert, and other partners. Through her company, she licenses goods such as accessories and linens.

Claiborne began by designing only dresses, but expanded to sportswear and petites. Children's wear and menswear have recently been added. She is known for her unusual color combinations, coordinate styling, and designs for working women.

OSCAR DE LA RENTA

1932 to
American designer

Born in the Dominican Republic, de la Renta studied art in Madrid and worked for Balenciaga shortly thereafter. He worked for designers in Paris and in New York before opening his own design company in 1965. Through his company, he licenses such products as furs and linens.

De la Renta was married to the former editor of French *Vogue*, Françoise de Langlade, until her death in 1984.

Romantically feminine evening gowns are a de la Renta trademark, as well as ruffles and bold striking colors, including black and white.

CHRISTIAN DIOR

1905 to 1957
French designer

Dior, credited with bringing elegance and grace back to women's dress after World War II, loved to sketch as a young boy. In school, he was punished for doodling ladies' feet in high-heels in his notebook margins.

As a young man, Dior studied political science and musical composition. Later, he made his living by selling fashion sketches. He eventually went to work designing for Piguet and Lelong. After serving in the French military, he and a friend opened an art gallery in 1928. After receiving advice from two fortunetellers, he opened his couture house in 1946.

Among Dior's innovations were the New Look following World War II, Gibson Girl blouses, neck to hem back-button detailing, low-cut necklines, Envol skirt, scissor skirts, evening dresses with bustle-like fullness, the A-line, the H-line, and the Y-line.

The Dior house was headed by Yves Saint Laurent on Dior's death in 1957. The house has been headed by Marc Bohan since 1960.

PERRY ELLIS

1940 to
American designer

Famous for his use of natural fibers in neutral colors, Ellis began his career as a retail buyer for Miller and Rhoads. He left retail to become a colorist and design assistant for sportswear manufacturer, John Meyer. In 1974, he became vice-president of merchandising for Vera, Inc. and eventually moved from merchandising to design. Manhattan Industries, the owners of Vera, Inc., launched his solo career with a design company known as Perry Ellis.

In 1976, *Women's Wear Daily* recognized Ellis' talent in an article entitled "On Their Way," which featured Ellis and four other designers.

Ellis' design contributions include dimple-sleeve jackets, baby cable-knit sweaters, cropped pants, boxy jackets, long, lean skirts, oversized sweaters atop full mini skirts, puffed shoulders, textured stockings, and wide waistbands.

GIANFRANCO FERRE

1944 to
Italian designer

The fact that Ferre studied architecture is evident in his architectural, yet fluid fashion designs. He began in the fashion industry by designing sculptured jewelry and then branched out into women's fashions. *W* magazine said of Ferre designs: "his clothes take the form of an elegantly balanced composition."

Ferre's designs include a softly constructed blazer with a bow in back, low necklines, the slouch dress, pleated dolman sleeves, and a high-tech look.

JAMES GALANOS

1925 to
American designer

California-based Galanos studied fashion in New York and worked for designers in New York and Paris before assisting Jean Louis in costume design for films. He opened his own design business in 1953 and offers ready-to-wear as well as custom designs.

Galanos received much attention for the white ball gown featuring exquisite hand beading that he designed for first lady Nancy Reagan to wear to the 1981 inaugural ball. Other design contributions include exquisite detailing, chiffon dresses, tailored suits, accessories, hand bead work, hand pleating, and luxurious fabrics.

JEAN-PAUL GAUTIER

1953 to
French designer

Gautier was first hired by Cardin as an assistant designer at age 16. Later, he designed for the house of Patou before opening his own design business in 1977, where he designs for a younger market than most French couturiers.

Gautier's designs, which are considered tongue-in-cheek, include sweatshirt and lace evening gowns, dresses with overly exaggerated, pointed breasts, garments that fit too tightly, the Punk Look, and unisex styling.

RUDI GERNREICH

1922 to 1985
American designer

Austrian-born Gernreich began his career as a sketch artist in his aunt's couture salon. He later attended art school in Los Angeles and accepted a job selling fabric. He opened his own Los Angeles-based design firm in 1951.

Gernreich created an uproar with his topless bathing suit and see-through blouses. Other design contributions are the unstructured bathing suit and tight-fitting minidresses made of knit fabric.

HUBERT DE GIVENCHY

1927 to
French designer

After studying art, Givenchy worked for fashion designers Lelong and Schiaparelli and then opened his own business in 1952. He now licenses eyewear and hosiery through his company.

Givenchy's simple, elegant styles were best displayed by actress Audrey Hepburn, one of his numerous clients. He also designed her wardrobe for the film, *Funny Face*.

His contributions include quality craftsmanship, the Bettina dress (open neckline and large ruffled sleeves in a peasant style), fitted wool suits, and a tunic coat with full puffed sleeves.

MADAME GRÈS

Germaine Alix Barton Grès
1910 to
French designer

Madame Grès likes to keep her background a mystery. We don't know if Grès (her husband's name Serge spelled backwards) is her real name or a take-off on his name.

She began her career by studying sculpture, which is evident in her finely sculpted designs. Her first job in the fashion field was making muslin patterns for a French design house. She opened her own house in 1934 and is considered by some to make "the world's most exquisite evening dresses."[1]

Grès' designs include draped jersey evening gowns, fluid chiffon evening gowns, cowl necklines on dresses, dolman sleeves, and coats with a kimono influence.

HALSTON

Roy Halston Frowick
1932 to
American designer

Halston, designer for such celebrities as Elizabeth Taylor, Liza Minelli, and Lauren Bacall, supported himself in art school by designing and selling hats. His first job was designing hats with Lilly Daché in 1957, and he began designing ready-to-wear for Bergdorf-Goodman in 1960. In 1968, he opened his own design company which was sold to Norton Simon, Inc. in 1973. Halston purchased his company back from Simon in 1984.

Licensing is a lucrative business for Halston. Among his numerous licenses are handbags, scarves, fragrance, and cosmetics. In 1983, he signed a contract with the retail chain J.C. Penney to develop a Halston III line exclusively for them.

His designs include Jacqueline Kennedy's inaugural pillbox hat, one-shoulder evening gowns, scarf hats, cashmere dresses, halter necklines, asymmetrical necklines, wrap skirts, caftans, and clean, simple lines. He also developed the technique to sew Ultra-Suede®.

EDITH HEAD

1899 to 1981
American designer

Edith Head studied French, Spanish, and art while in college and later taught at an exclusive girls' school before accepting work as a sketch artist in Paramount Studios' costume department. She eventually became the head costume designer for Universal Studios.

Throughout her career, Head was honored with eight "Oscars" for her film costume design work.

She designed for such screen stars as Elizabeth Taylor, Mae West, Carole Lombard, Joan Crawford, Bette Davis, Grace Kelly, Ingrid Bergman, Paul Newman, and Robert Redford.

NORMA KAMALI

1945 to
American designer

Before attending New York's Fashion Institute of Technology, Norma Kamali studied painting and art history. Her first job after graduation was as a freelance fashion illustrator.

In the early 1960s, Kamali worked for an airline company and traveled continuously. Her travels often took her to London, a city that had a powerful effect on fashion in the 1960s and on Kamali as well. She returned to New York and opened her own shop in 1968 where she designed for rock stars, as well as for the public. After she divorced her husband in 1978, she opened a new shop called OMO—Norma Kamali (OMO meaning "on my own"). Through her company, she has licensed numerous products including hosiery, footwear, fragrance, cosmetics, and ready-to-wear.

Kamali is known for garments made of parachute cloth, sleeping bag coats, swimsuits featuring a high-cut leg, sweatshirt fleece garments, and large shoulder pads. She also designed the costumes for Raquel Welch in her Broadway show "Woman of the Year." She was the first designer to make use of videos to merchandise fashion garments.

KENZO

Kenzo Takada
1945 to
French designer

Japanese-born Kenzo entered the fashion world after graduating from Tokyo's Bunka College of Fashion. He began by designing patterns for a magazine. He opened his own design firm in Paris in 1971 and his first collection was pirated before his orders were delivered. But by the late 1970s, Kenzo was known in the fashion industry. He also opened a boutique called "Jungle Jap."

In 1983, Kenzo began a licensing agreement with The Limited, a juniors retail chain in the United States. Other licensing agreements include Butterick patterns and hosiery.

Kenzo's designs include kimono-shaped deep-shoulder knits; the layered look; oversized jackets and pants; mixing of florals, stripes, and plaids on the same garment; quilted cottons; and longer, wider skirts.

ANNE KLEIN

Hannah Golofski
1923 to 1974
American designer

Anne Klein began her career in fashion as a freelance sketcher in 1938 and began designing ten years later. She opened her own company, Anne Klein and Co., in 1968, and used the lion's head as her logo because her astrological sign was Leo. She made her earliest impact on the juniors market and later moved on to misses.

Since her death from pneumonia in 1974, Anne Klein and Co. has been headed by Klein's assistant, Donna Karan and Louis Dell 'Olio (a former classmate of Karan's). The company has had numerous licensing agreements including eyewear, shoes, and linens. Karan surprised the fashion industry in 1984 when she announced she would leave Anne Klein and Co. to start her own company and act as an occasional consultant to Dell 'Olio.

The designs of Anne Klein and Co. have included clean lines, classic styling, jersey evening dresses featuring attached hoods, wasp-waisted dresses with full skirts, blazers topping plaid, pleated skirts, leather garments, and the chemise.

CALVIN KLEIN

1942 to
American designer

After graduating from New York's Fashion Institute of Technology, Klein apprenticed for a New York-based coat and suit manufacturer for five years.

In 1968, he and his lifelong friend, Barry Schwartz, began a coat designing company known as Calvin Klein, Ltd. Their first order was placed with Bonwit Teller for $50,000. Klein soon expanded his designs to add women's and men's fashions. Through his company, he licenses products including fragrances, cosmetics, and children's wear.

Klein signed a licensing agreement with Puritan in the late 1970s. This joint venture created the Calvin Klein jean, making Klein a household name to millions. He eventually bought the Puritan Corporation and added it to his holdings.

Known for designs using natural fibers in warm tones, sophisticated sportswear, architectural suits, and simple, classic lines, Klein was the youngest designer to ever win the Coty Award, at age 31. He is also the first designer to win the Coty Award three consecutive years. (The Coty award is an award given annually to top American designers in various fashion categories.)

KARL LAGERFELD

1939 to
French designer

German-born Lagerfeld relocated to Paris in 1953 to pursue his dream and become a fashion designer. Two years later he received his first design award.

Initially a designer for the House of Chloé, Lagerfeld has expanded to other avenues. In 1982, he became head designer for the House of Chanel, in addition to designing for his own label and designing furs for Fendi of Rome.

Lagerfeld is known for innovative proportions, cottons featuring exquisite detailed embroidery, short skirts, fluid lines, and adding his touch of wit to the classic Chanel suit.

RALPH LAUREN

Ralph Lipshetz
1939 to
American designer

While attending business courses in the evening, Lauren worked at Brooks Brothers selling ties and later became an assistant buyer for a retail store. He left retail to work as a necktie designer for Beau Brummel, Inc. under the label "Polo." In 1968, he began his own company, under the name Polo, where he designed mens-wear. Three years later, he added women's wear, followed by boy's wear and many licenses including linens, fragrances, and cosmetics. In addition to Polo, he also has lines known as Chaps and Ralph Lauren Designs.

Lauren is known for wide neckties for men, silk tweed jackets over floral chintz skirts, the Ivy League preppy look, western wear, the prairie look, the English aristocracy look, and sporty, yet romantic styling. He also designed uniforms for Transworld Airlines. In addition, he has designed men's wardrobes for films including *The Great Gatsby* and *Annie Hall*.

BOB MACKIE

1940 to
American designer

After graduating from art school, Mackie worked as a design assistant for Edith Head. In 1963, he was hired as an assistant designer to Ray Aghayan on Judy Garland's television show. With Aghayan, he also designed for films including *Lady Sings the Blues* and *Funny Lady*. Mackie eventually branched out on his own and designed for television shows including *The Sonny and Cher Show, The Carol Burnett Show, The Donny and Marie Osmond Show,* and many television specials.

He licensed lingerie in the late 1970s and introduced an elegant ready-to-wear line in the early 1980s, featuring his famous style of bugle beading.

MARIUCCIA MANDELLI

Birthdate unavailable
Italian designer

Mandelli, a former grade school teacher, began her company known as Krizia in 1954 with money that her sister gave her from hocking her motorcycle. The name "Krizia" was taken from one of Plato's dialogues on women's vanities.

Mandelli uses animals for her design signature. She introduces a different species in each season's collection, from bears to dalmations. Her design innovations have included hot pants, midi and maxi skirts, elegantly tailored suits for women fashioned from menswear fabrics, square-shouldered cashmere capes, cellophane dresses tiered like New York's Chrysler Building, and coatdresses.

In 1985, she signed a licensing agreement with The Limited, a United States juniors chain, to create an exclusive line for the store.

JESSICA McCLINTOCK

1931 to
American designer

San Francisco-based McClintock left her job teaching school to begin her design career. She now designs for two lines—Gunne Sax (juniors) and Jessica McClintock (misses).

McClintock has inspired looks including romantic dresses with lace, dropped waistlines, lace collars, silk charmeuse evening dresses, bridal wear, and calico fabrics.

MARY McFADDEN

1936 to
American designer

McFadden, after studying design in New York and France, was hired as public relations director for Dior's New York branch in 1962. In 1964, she moved with her husband to South Africa and became the editor of *Vogue—South Africa* until the magazine was discontinued the next year. On returning to the United States in 1970, she worked as editor of special projects for *Vogue*. In her spare time, McFadden designed and constructed tunics of hand-painted silks which were purchased by retailer, Henri Bendel. Her design business was launched in 1976. Through her business she licenses products including fragrances, jewelry, and home decorating items. She also signed a licensing agreement in 1985 to design garments for J.C. Penney, Inc.

While in Africa, McFadden became interested in symbols from ancient cultures. In each of her collections, she translates an historical period through her designs. This is reflected in her garments that feature luxurious fabrics, pleating, fabric braids and ropes attached to garments, and hand-painted silks.

NOLAN MILLER

1936 to
American designer

As a youngster, Miller would get into trouble for sketching garments during algebra exams. Raised in Texas, he relocated to Los Angeles and graduated from the Chouinard Art Institute. He couldn't find a job in design, so he worked for a Beverly Hills florist. It was in the florist shop that he met producer Aaron Spelling, who hired him to design costumes for a television western. In 1957, he continued to design for television while he opened his own design studio in Beverly Hills.

Miller has become well known to the public as the fashion designer for television shows such as *Dynasty, Hotel, Matt Houston,* and *Love Boat.* His licensing agreements include a *Dynasty* ready-to-wear collection and a *Dynasty* lingerie collection.

ISSEY MIYAKE

1938 to
Japanese designer

Miyake began showing under his own name in 1971, after studying art in Tokyo and serving apprenticeships with Beene in New York and Givenchy and Guy Laroche in Paris.

He is known for using sashiko, the quilted fabric used for many generations in Japanese workers' garments and judo uniforms. Miyake's design innovations have included the mixing of Oriental ingenuity with Western tailoring, the bamboo bodice, bright red plastic bustier, neutral colors, layering of garments, wire bustier, draped skirts, textured knits, and a free, loose fit.

CLAUDE MONTANA

1949 to
French designer

As a youth, Montana was rebellious and disliked school as well as studying. At first, he wanted a career in archeology. He ran away from home at age 17 to work for the Paris Opera as an extra. Five years later, he relocated to London, where he designed papier-maché jewelry. He returned to Paris the following year and worked as a design assistant for a leather fashion manufacturer.

Eventually, Montana began his own design company where he creates a men's and a women's ready-to-wear line as well as a line for the Italian company, Complice.

Montana, who first made his name with machismo-flavored bikers' leathers for women,[2] is also known for military fashions, nautical looks, oversized football jerseys, overly exaggerated pinstripe Wall Street suits for women, and large shoulder interest.

PAUL POIRET

1879 to 1944
French designer

Poiret opened his own shop in 1904 after working as an umbrella shop assistant, sketch artist, and apprentice to designer Jacques Doucet and the House of Worth. His wife Denise was his model. Tall and thin, she was envisioned by Poiret as the woman of the future and he set out to "create her."

Considered one of the greatest designers of all time, Poiret is known for persuading women to give up wearing corsets. He is also known for Greek-inspired fashions, the empire waistline, simplified garments, the girdle, the sack gown, the hobble skirt, the lampshade gown, slit skirts, turbans, Orient-inspired fashions, the Russian tunic coat, and the use of egret feathers on his fashions.

MARY QUANT

1934 to
British designer

Quant opened "Bazaar," her small boutique in the Chelsea district of London, after studying art at Goldsmith's College.

Known as the fashion innovator for youth in the 1960s, with the "Mod" look, Quant is also known for designs such as the mini skirt, large sweaters worn over skin-tight pants, knickers, hiphugger pants, colored tights, and thick, opaque legwear.

Endnotes

CHAPTER 1

1. T. Berry Brazelton, "What Do Newborns Really See?," *Redbook's Young Mother,* 1977, pp. 28–29.
2. Faber Birren, *Light, Color and Environment* (New York: Van Nostrand Reinhold Co., 1969), pp. 30–31.
3. Ibid., p. 19.
4. The Impressionists, a school of painters that developed in France in the 1870s, used unmixed colors and small brush strokes to create the effect of luminosity. Monet was an Impressionist.
5. Old Masters refers to the distinguished artists of the sixteenth, seventeenth, or early eighteenth century. Rembrandt was an Old Master.

CHAPTER 4

1. Sharon Lee Tate and Mona Shafer Edwards, *The Fashion Coloring Book* (New York: Harper & Row, 1984), p. 134.

CHAPTER 5

1. Evelyn Oliver, *Fashion Is History* (Sacramento, California: Bottaro Ltd., 1981), p. 17.
2. Ibid., p. 19.
3. Marybelle S. Bigelow, *Fashion In History,* 2nd ed. (Minneapolis: Burgess Publishing Co., 1979), p. 150.
4. Ibid., p. 152.

5. Blanche Payne, *History of Costume* (New York: Harper & Row, 1965), p. 355.
6. Mila Contini, *Fashion* (New York: Crescent Books, 1965), pp. 149–150.
7. Evelyn Oliver, *Fashion Is History* (Sacramento, California: Bottaro Ltd., 1981), p. 36.
8. Michael and Ariane Batterberry, *Mirror Mirror* (New York: Holt, Rinehart, and Winston, 1977).
9. Evelyn Oliver, *Fashion Is History* (Sacramento, California: Bottaro Ltd., 1981), p. 42.
10. Ellen Melinkoff, *What We Wore* (New York: Quill, 1984), pp. 111–112.

CHAPTER 6

1. *W,* "The 24 Greatest," November 30 to December 7, 1984, p. 72.
2. *W,* "I, Claude," June 15 to 22, 1984, p. 9.

Bibliography

Anderson, Donald M. *Elements of Design.* New York: Holt, Rinehart and Winston, 1961.

August, Bonnie, and Ellen Court. *The Complete Bonnie August Dress Thin System.* New York: Rawson, Wade Publishers, Inc., 1981.

Bailey, Margaret J. *Those Glorious Glamour Years.* Secaucus, N. J.: The Citadel Press, 1982.

Bates, Kenneth F. *Basic Design: Principles and Practice.* New York: Funk & Wagnalls, 1975.

Batterberry, Michael, and Ariane Batterberry. *Mirror Mirror.* New York: Holt, Rinehart and Winston, 1977.

Bell, Quentin. *On Human Finery,* 2nd ed. New York: Schocken Books, 1978.

Bernier, Olivier. *The Eighteenth Century Woman.* Garden City, N.Y.: Doubleday and Company, Inc., 1981.

Bigelow, Marybelle S. *Fashion in History,* 2nd ed. Minneapolis: Burgess Publishing Company, 1979.

Birren, Faber. *A Grammar of Color.* New York: Van Nostrand Reinhold Co., 1969.

Birren, Faber. *Color in Your World.* New York: Macmillan Co., 1966.

Birren, Faber. *Color Psychology and Color Therapy.* New Hyde Park, New York: Citadel Press, 1978.

Birren, Faber. *Creative Color.* New York: Van Nostrand Reinhold Co., 1961.

Birren, Faber. *Light, Color and Environment.* New York: Van Nostrand Reinhold Co., 1969.

Birren, Faber. *Principles of Color.* New York: Van Nostrand Reinhold Co., 1969.

Birren, Faber. *Selling Color to People.* New York: Van Nostrand Reinhold Co., 1956.

Birren, Faber. *The Color Primer: A Basic Treatise on the Color System of Wilhelm Ostwald.* New York: Van Nostrand Reinhold Co., 1969.

Boucher, Francois. *20,000 Years of Fashion.* New York: Harry N. Abrams, Inc.

Brazelton, T. Berry. "What Do Newborns Really See?" *Redbook's Young Mother,* 1977, pp. 28–29.

Brubach, Holly. "Perry Ellis: An American Original." *Vogue,* August 1980.

Carter, Ernestine. *Magic Names of Fashion.* Englewood Cliffs, N.J.: Prentice-Hall, Inc., 1980.

Charles-Roux, Edmonde. *Chanel and Her World.* London: Weidenfeld and Nicolson, 1981.

Cho, Emily, and Linda Grover. *Looking Terrific.* New York: G. P. Putnam's Sons, 1978.

Cocks, Jay. "Into the Soul of Fashion." *Time,* August 1, 1983.

Contini, Mila. *Fashion.* New York: Crescent Books, 1965.

Devlin, Polly. *Vogue Book of Fashion Photography 1919 to 1979.* New York: Simon and Schuster, 1979.

Dilley, Romilda. *Drawing Women's Fashions.* New York: Watson-Guptill Publications, 1959.

Dorner, Jane. *Fashion.* New York: Octopus Books Limited, 1974.

Dryansky, G. Y. "By Design: A World Called Cardin." *Vogue,* July 1982.

Erwin, Mabel D., Lila A. Kinchen, and Kathleen A. Peters. *Clothing For Moderns,* 6th ed. New York: Macmillan Publishing Co., Inc., 1979.

Ewing, Elizabeth. *History of 20th Century Fashion.* London: Batsford, Ltd., 1974.

Fabri, Ralph. *Color: A Complete Guide for Artists.* New York: Watson-Guptill Publications, 1967.

Fairchild, John. *The Fashionable Savages.* Garden City, N.Y.: Doubleday and Co., Inc., 1965.

Fashion Dictionary: Fabric, Sewing, and Apparel As Expressed in the Language of Fashion, ed. by Mary Brooks Picken. New York: Funk & Wagnalls, 1972.

Flusser, Alan. *Making the Man.* New York: Simon and Schuster, 1981.

Gorsline, Douglas. *What People Wore.* New York: Bonanza Books, 1962.

Gross, Edith Loew. "Bill Blass and Women: An American Affair." *Vogue,* March 1981.

Head, Edith, and Paddy Calistro. *Edith Head's Hollywood.* New York: E. P. Dutton, Inc., 1983.

Houck, Catherine. *The Fashion Encyclopedia.* New York: St. Martin's Press, 1982.

"I, Claude." *W,* June 15 to June 22, 1984.

Ireland, Patrick John. *Fashion Design Drawing.* New York: Halstead Press, 1975.

Ireland, Patrick John. *Fashion Drawing for Advertising.* New York: John Wiley & Sons, 1974.

Jackson, Carole. *Color Me Beautiful.* Washington: Acropolis Books Ltd., 1980.

Keenan, Brigid. *Dior in Vogue.* New York: Harmony Books, 1981.

Kennett, Frances. *Secrets of the Couturiers.* London: Orbis Publishing, Ltd., 1984.

La Vine, W. Robert. *In a Glamorous Fashion.* New York: Charles Scribner's Sons, 1980.

Lenker, Sandra. *Vogue Fitting.* New York: Harper & Row, 1984.

Mackie, Bob. *Dressing for Glamour.* New York: A and W Press, 1979.

McConathy, Dale, and Diana Vreeland. *Hollywood Costume.* New York: Harry N. Abrams, Inc., 1976.

Melinkoff, Ellen. *What We Wore.* New York: Quill Publications, 1984.

Metropolitan Museum of Art. *The Imperial Style: Fashions of the Hapsburg Era.* New York: Rizzoli Publishing, 1980.

Oliver, Evelyn. *Fashion Is History.* Sacramento: Bottaro, Ltd., 1981.

Morse, Patricia. *Needleart.* Elk Grove, California: Morse Publishers, 1984.

Payne, Blanche. *History of Costume.* New York: Harper & Row, 1965.

Peck, Stephen Rogers. *Atlas of Human Anatomy for the Artist.* New York: Oxford University Press, 1951.

Reader's Digest Complete Guide to Sewing, ed. by Virginia Colton. New York: The Reader's Digest Association, Inc., 1976.

Saint Laurent, Yves. *Yves Saint Laurent.* New York: Clarkson N. Potter, Inc., 1983.

Sargent, Walter. *The Enjoyment and Use of Color.* New York: Dover Publications, 1964.

Selbie, Robert. *The Anatomy of Costume.* New York: Crescent Books, 1977.

Sheppard, Joseph. *Drawing the Male Figure.* Cincinnati, Ohio: Watson-Guptill, 1976.

Stegemeyer, Anne. *Who's Who in Fashion.* New York: Fairchild Publications, 1980.

Tate, Sharon Lee, and Mona Shafer Edwards. *The Fashion Coloring Book.* New York: Harper & Row, 1984.

Tate, Sharon Lee. *Inside Fashion Design,* 2nd ed. New York: Harper & Row, 1984.

Taylor, F. A. *Colour Technology.* London: Oxford University Press, 1962.

"They All Wore Dresses By Adrian." *The San Francisco Chronicle,* July 15, 1978.

"The 24 Greatest." *W,* November 30 to December 7, 1984.

Wilcox, R. Turner. *The Dictionary of Costume.* New York: Charles Scribner's Sons, 1963.

Wingate, Isabel B., Karen R. Gillespie, and Betty G. Addison. *Know Your Merchandise,* 4th ed. New York: McGraw-Hill Book Co., 1975.

Worthington, Christa. "Three Decades of Krizia." *Women's Wear Daily,* February 28, 1984.

Index

French Revolution, influence of, 78–79
French seam, 42
French Vogue (magazine), 103
Frock coat, 82
Frog, 40
Frowick, Roy Halston, 99
Full-fashioned garment, 40
Full-front figure drawing, 54–62
Funny Face (movie), 98
Funny Lady (movie), 101

Galanos, James, 98
Galeries Lafayette, 103
Garbo, Greta, 94
Garland, Judy, 94
Gates ajar, 82
Gathering, 40
Gaucho pants, 27
Gautier, Jean-Paul, 98
Gaynor, Janet, 94
Gernreich, Rudi, 89, 98
Gibson, Charles Dana, 84
Gibson Girl, 84, 85
   blouses, 97
Gimp, 40
Givenchy, Hubert de, 95, 98–99, 102
Godet, 40
   skirt, 16
Godey's Lady's Book, 82
Gore, 40
Gored skirt or dress, 14, 16
Gothic architecture, influence of, 72
Graduated rhythm, 49
Grain, 40
Grease (movie), 91
Greatcoat, 20
Great Gatsby, The (movie), 100
Greeks
   costume history of, 68–69, 70
   influence of, 80–84
Greenburg, Adrian Adolph, 94
Grès, Madame (Germaine Alix Barton), 14, 98
Gunna, 71–72
Gunne Sax dresses, 90, 101
Gusset, 40

Hacking jacket, 24
Hairstyles, 78, 80–81
Half-size figure, 62
Halston, 98–99
Halter, 30
"Handkerchief" hemline, 85
Harem pants, 27
Harlow, Jean, 68, 85
Harmony, 49
Harris, Upham, & Company, 66
Hat, picture, 84. *See also* Accessories
Hawaiian shirt, 16–17
Head, Edith, 99, 101
Headrails, 72
Hem, 40
Hemlines, 66, 85, 86, 89
Hendrix, Jimi, 89
Hennin, 72–74
Henri Bendel, 101

Hepburn, Audrey, 86–88, 98
Heraldry, 74
Hering, Ewald, 10
High neckline, 30
High Renaissance costume, 74–76, 77
Himation, 69, 71
Hip-hugger style, 27, 89
Hippie Look, 89, 90
History of costume. *See* Costume history
H-line style, 88, 97
Hobble skirt, 84–85, 86
Hook and eye, 40
Horizontal lines, 46
Hornsby, Lesley "Twiggy," 89
Hosiery, 72, 74, 76. *See also* Accessories
Hotel (TV), 102
Hot pants, 89–90
Hourglass figure, 84
Hourglass suit, 20, 23
Hue, 10, 11

I.M. International, 94
Illness associated with colors, 2
Image, customer, 62–65
Incroyables, 79
Indispensables, 80
Informal balance, 49, 51
Inter-Color, 9
Interfacing, 40
Interlining, 40
Intermediate colors, 9–10
Inverted pleats, 42
Iridescence effects, color and, 11
Italy, master tailoring of, 91, 92
Ives, Herbert E., 11
Ivy League look, 27, 88

J.C. Penney, Inc., 99, 101
Jabot, 30, 78
Jackets, fashion details of, 20–25
   Spencer, 24, 79, 80
Jackson, Michael, 68, 91
Jazz, Age of, 85
Jeans, 27, 89, 90, 100
Jefferson Airplane, 89
Jerkin, 74
Jewel neckline, 31
Jodhpurs, 27
Jogging suit, 21, 23
John Meyer, 97
Johnny collar, 30
Joplin, Janis, 89
Josephine, Empress, 82
Jumper, 17
Jumpsuit, 27, 29
"Jungle Jap," 99
Junior size, 62
Justaucorps, 78, 79

Kalasiris, 68, 69
Kamali, Norma, 47, 91, 99–100, 107
Keaton, Diane, 68
Kelly, Grace, 99
Kennedy, Jacqueline, 66, 88, 89, 99
Kenzo, 99